THE PORTSMOUTH FC MISCELLANY

POMPEY HISTORY, TRIVIA, FACTS & STATS

ROGER HOLMES

THE PORTSMOUTH FC MISCELLANY
POMPEY HISTORY, TRIVIA, FACTS & STATS

All statistics, facts and figures are correct as of 1st August 2006

© Roger Holmes

Roger Holmes has asserted his rights in accordance with the Copyright, Designs and Patents Act 1988 to be identified as the author of this work.

Published By:
Pitch Publishing (Brighton) Ltd
10 Beresford Court
Somerhill Road
Hove BN3 1RH

Email: info@pitchpublishing.co.uk
Web: www.pitchpublishing.co.uk

First published 2006

A catalogue record for this book is available from the British Library.

10-digit ISBN: 1-9054110-1-4
13-digit ISBN: 978-1-9054110-1-6

Printed and bound in Great Britain by Cromwell Press

FOREWORD BY GUY WHITTINGHAM

BY LATTER DAY standards I came to the professional game rather late having been plucked by Portsmouth Football Club from a budding career in the army, at a cost of £450, in my 24th year. I shall always be grateful to the club for offering me the chance to prosper at a game that I loved, and where I spent the best moments of my playing career. When I finally retired from the game I could look back with pride on the fact that I held the goal scoring record for Pompey of 42 goals in the 1992-3 season – a record which, given the tightness of modern defences, may be difficult to surpass! Not surprisingly therefore, I was delighted to be asked by Roger to write the foreword to this intriguing take on the history of Portsmouth Football Club. Reading it not only rekindled fond and personal memories of former times spent with great team mates, but it also brought into focus the colourful and lasting contributions made to the history of the club by players, officials, fans and commentators over many decades.

Set out in easily digestible bites, we come upon references to the longest, best or highest mingled with the capricious, the curious, and even the poignant, the latter reminding us that whatever the game has become, football has always had a heart. In short, Roger has produced a book that is easy to read, and difficult to put down, a "must have" for the Pompey faithful, with a sufficiently sympathetic text to capture the imagination of the as yet uncommitted. If you want to know anything about Portsmouth Football Club, chances are you will find it here, and I wish Roger every success with the book.

Guy Whittingham
Portsmouth FC, 1989-93 and 1999-2001

INTRODUCTION

AS THOSE SIX enterprising Victorian Founding Fathers were casting their eye, towards the end of the nineteenth century, over the four and a half acres of cow-strewn agricultural land close to Goldsmith Avenue, they would hardly have imagined the true significance of their commendable vision. From this piece of land, which they purchased, landscaped and developed would emerge an embryonic Portsmouth Football Club and a playing surface that would in time become its spiritual home, and Mecca to football mad youngsters and their elders – Fratton Park. Throughout the ensuing century the club's triumphs and adversities, trials and tribulations have captivated not only generations of local enthusiasts, but also, reflecting no doubt the city's military and naval historical roots, a following beyond its south-coast boundaries.

Before I had even mastered the skill of joined-up writing, I was already steeped in Pompey football folklore, beguiled as I was by tales told and retold by my football-mad father and grandfathers – a family tradition which survives to this day. Had my grandmother's admonition that they cease filling my head "with all that rubbish" been heeded, this, and my first book *Pompey Players*, would never have seen the light of day. It was while spooling through the annals of Portsmouth Football Club that I began to gather together not only a myriad assortment of historical facts and figures, but also a veritable cascade of bizarre events and other interesting trivia, amounting to a treasure trove of material that was difficult to resist!

The result is a kind of manual, the overall aim of which has been to encapsulate the more appealing events in the club's history – and the selection process did offer quite a challenge – in a form which would be easy on the eye and which might invite both serious and casual exploration. So, whereas the chronology of promotion and relegation statistics for example, has been preserved, the randomly placed in-fills of the hitherto unknown, the amusing snippet or the quirky happening help to justify the miscellany of the title.

My life-long interest in the affairs of Portsmouth Football Club, which has cemented its pivotal role in the life of the community, has provided me, and no doubt scores of others, with pleasure and pain in almost equal measure – the universal fate of the true football fanatic! There have been times when the affairs of the club have assumed soap opera proportions, or the topsy turvy plot of a Gilbert and Sullivan comic opera – and coincidentally, namesakes of theirs were once on the club's playing staff at the same time! I hope that this book will provide both pleasure and source material for anyone seeking them, but especially for the committed fan who, like me, must surely be on the cusp of anorak sainthood. I hope too that my grandmother would have approved!

Roger Holmes, October 2006

FORMATION OF PORTSMOUTH FOOTBALL CLUB

Portsmouth Football Club was formed on 5 April 1898, when a group of businessmen and legal people formed a syndicate. Fratton Park was purchased for £4,950, and a limited company was registered. The ground was farmland, used largely as a market garden. The prospectus of the new company was prepared and advertised, with a capital of £8,000 divided into £1 shares. The prospectus set forth that, "the company was formed for the purpose of acquiring and laying out of a piece of land with an acreage of four-and-a-half acres situated at Goldsmith Avenue, Fratton to be used primarily for the game of football and also for other games and exercises as shall be decided on by the directors from time to time."

WEDDING DAY DASH

On 12 April 1958, Ray Crawford made a car dash from his wedding at St Mary's Church, Portsea, to Fratton Park. He played at outside-left in Pompey's 2-1 defeat against Blackpool and, after the match, rejoined his wedding guests at the reception.

ONLY LEEDS COULDN'T SCORE

When Pompey beat Leeds United 2-0 at Fratton Park on 11 October 1958, it was the only occasion during the 1958/59 season that they kept a clean sheet in a league match.

THE FIRST SUBSTITUTES

Tony Barton was the first ever used Pompey substitute. He replaced injured Vince Radcliffe during a 2-2 draw with Southampton at The Dell on 28 August 1965. The first Pompey sub to score was Mick Travers, who netted in a 3-1 home win over Blackpool on 2 December 1967.

MATCH OF THE DAY

Pompey's first appearance on BBC Match of the Day was on 25 February 1967. They lost a Second Division clash 3-2 at home to promotion-chasing Wolverhampton Wanderers after leading 2-0 at half-time, with Cliff Portwood scoring both goals.

LONG THROW

Roy Lunniss, a Pompey full-back between 1963 and 1966, was well known for taking long throw-ins. His throw was measured at 37yds 2ft 6ins.

LOCAL BOY MAKES GOOD

On 19 April 1939, 19-year-old Reg Flewin was the first Portsmouth-born player to appear in Pompey's League side since the club became members of the Football League in 1920. He played at centre-half in a 2-1 victory at home to Grimsby Town. This was his only league outing before war broke out, and he is the last surviving first-team player from Pompey's pre-war days.

RECORD TRANSFERS

Pompey broke their transfer record four times within 12 months. On 27 December 1972, Bobby Kellard rejoined the club from Crystal Palace for £42,000. In May 1973, Phil Roberts switched from Bristol Rovers for £55,000, and within days Pompey made their first £100,000 signing when Peter Marinello moved from Arsenal. The record transfer fee was shattered again on 6 December 1973, with Paul Went leaving Fulham for £154,000. This fee remained the club's highest transfer fee paid for the best part of ten years – it was broken when Mark Hateley signed from Coventry City for £190,000 in May 1983.

TAYLOR MADE

Bristol Rovers left-back Tony Taylor applied to become Pompey's first-team coach in January 1978, but the job was given to Frank Burrows. The new appointment immediately began to help manager Jimmy Dickinson with the acquisition of new players, and the first player to sign was Tony Taylor, six days almost to the minute after he was interviewed for the coaching position.

TOO MUCH TO SAY

Duggie Reid was a man of few words, but once talked himself out of the team. In April 1951, he approached manager Bob Jackson and said, "Do you realise that Len Phillips' best position is at inside-right?" Jackson thought it over, moved Phillips to the inside-right position for the final two matches of the season, and dropped Reid to the reserves.

EVER PRESENT ERNIE

Goalkeeper Ernie Butler was the only player to appear in all Pompey's league and cup matches during the League Championship-winning seasons of 1948/49 and 1949/50. Ironically, he missed the first match of the 1950/51 campaign because of a dislocated finger.

HOLDING THE CUP

Mrs Gladys Smith claimed she held the FA Cup more than anybody! She joined the Fratton Park staff in 1930 as matchday hostess, and worked at the ground during the week as a cleaner and laundry woman. During the Second World War, one of her jobs was to polish the FA Cup trophy, which was won by Pompey in 1939. As the competition was suspended until 1946, the cup remained at Fratton Park throughout the hostilities, and so Mrs Smith's claim is almost certain to be true. She was still working for the club when she died in 1978.

HIGHEST RESERVE ATTENDANCE

On 1 March 1952 at Fratton Park, a record reserve crowd of 30,289 watched Pompey Reserves thrash Charlton Athletic's second string 5-1 in a London Combination fixture. The reason for this huge attendance was that tickets for the following week's FA Cup quarter-final clash at home to Newcastle United were on sale.

PROUD HOME RECORD

Pompey dropped only three points as they remained unbeaten at Fratton Park throughout the 1948/49 campaign. They triumphed in 18 of the 21 league fixtures at Fratton Park, and won all four of their FA Cup-ties. Blackpool, Bolton Wanderers, and Manchester United were the three teams to return home with a point.

BEAT POMPEY AND YOU WIN THE CUP

Three times in five years the team that knocked Pompey out of the FA Cup went on to lift the trophy. In 1967, Tottenham Hotspur beat Pompey 3-1 at White Hart Lane in the fourth round, and won 2-1 against Chelsea in the final. A year later, West Bromwich Albion recorded a 2-1 victory at Fratton Park in the fifth round, and went on to beat Everton 1-0 at Wembley. In 1971, Pompey held Arsenal to a 1-1 draw at Fratton Park in Round Four, but lost 3-2 at Highbury in the replay. The Gunners defeated Liverpool 2-1 in the final.

PLAYED AND MANAGED

Six men have played league football for Pompey and also managed the club. They are Bill Thompson (caretaker), Ron Tindall, Jimmy Dickinson, Bobby Campbell, Tony Barton (caretaker) and Steve Claridge (player-manager).

POMPEY STILL WAITING TO KNOCK OUT SAINTS

Pompey have yet to beat Southampton in a major cup competition. They were first drawn together in the first round of the FA Cup in 1906, when Saints won 5-1 at The Dell. Remarkably, they didn't meet again until 1984 when, at Fratton Park, a last-minute goal by Steve Moran was enough to knock Pompey out of the cup in the fourth round. In 1996, Saints won an FA Cup third round tie 3-0 at The Dell, and they also won 2-1 at St. Mary's in the fourth round in January 2005. So far, the two clubs have met just once in the League Cup – in December 2003, when Southampton won the fourth round tie 2-0.

THE FIRST SUNDAY SINNERS

Pompey's Bobby Kellard was the first player ever to be sent off on a Sunday in a professional match in England. He was ordered off during the 1-1 draw between Pompey and West Bromwich Albion at Fratton Park on 3 February 1974. Albion's David Shaw also received his marching orders later in the game.

FIRST TIME AT THE TOP

Pompey went top of Division One for the first time on 10 September 1932 by beating Wolverhampton Wanderers 2-0 at Fratton Park. Jack Smith scored with seven minutes to go, then Jimmy Allen made sure of victory with a header.

WORLD CUP MISSERS

Two of England's 1966 World Cup Final winners have missed penalties at Fratton Park. In April 1963, central defender Jack Charlton saw his effort saved by John Armstrong in Pompey's 3-0 win over Leeds United, and in January 1981 midfielder Alan Ball was unsuccessful whilst playing for Blackpool in a 3-3 draw. His shot hit the post, and he slammed home the rebound, but as the ball had not touched another player the goal was disallowed.

SEVEN TIMES BEATEN

Players who have a testimonial game usually enjoy the match and end up on the winning side. Not so John Milkins. In May 1972, the Pompey goalkeeper was rewarded for his long service at Fratton Park with a testimonial match against Southampton, but had to pick the ball out of the net seven times as Saints ran out 7-0 winners.

THREE POINTS

Three points, instead of two, for a win was introduced at the start of the 1981/82 season to encourage more attacking football. Pompey had to wait until their sixth league match to collect their first three points, winning 2-0 away to Oxford United in a Division Three fixture.

FIRST LEAGUE HAT TRICK

The first Pompey player to score a hat trick in the Football League was Percy Cherrett; he netted three times in the 4-1 home win over Gillingham in October 1921 in a Division Three (South) fixture.

TOP MARKSMEN

Two Pompey players have led their divisional goalscoring charts. Ron Saunders topped the Second Division with 33 league goals in 1963/64 and the 1992/93 campaign saw Guy Whittingham lead the First Division scoring charts with 42.

RECORD CUP VICTORY

The 10-0 thrashing of Ryde in their first FA Cup tie on 30 September 1899 remains Pompey's biggest victory in the competition. Pompey were at that time obliged to play through the qualifying stages of the English Cup, as it was then known, and they defeated Cowes, Swindon, Bristol Rovers, and Bedminster before meeting Blackburn Rovers in the first round. They drew twice with the Lancashire club before losing 5-0 in the second replay.

THE SHANKLY CONNECTION

Robert Blyth, the uncle of legendary Liverpool manager Bill Shankly, served Portsmouth Football Club as player, captain, manager, director, vice-chairman, and chairman. He captained Pompey in their very first competitive match, and made 175 appearances before becoming manager in 1901, guiding the team to the Southern League championship in his first year. He joined the board of directors in 1909, and was chairman from September 1924 until August 1934. The family connection continued when his son Bob scored twice in eight league appearances during the 1921/22 campaign before moving to Southampton. Two of Bill Shankly's four brothers, John and Jimmy, were also on Pompey's books, and played regularly for the reserves, but only John played in the first team, making three appearances in 1923.

HIRON'S FAVOURITE OPPONENTS

Ray Hiron seemed to enjoy Carlisle United's visits to Fratton Park. He scored in every one of the six meetings between the two sides from 1965/66 to 1970/71.

SATURDAY MAN

David Kemp scored for Pompey on ten consecutive Saturdays during the 1977/78 season, starting on 24 September when he grabbed the only goal away to Exeter City, and completing the run on 19 November, when he netted in a 2-0 home win over Hereford United.

TOP FIVE FA CUP GOALSCORERS

The top five Pompey goalscorers in the FA Cup are:

Peter Harris 15
Johnny Weddle 12
Guy Whittingham 10
Ron Saunders 9
Billy Haines 8

HEAVY POST-WAR DEFEATS

Pompey have been beaten 7-0 three times since the war, but on 27 November 1965, they conceded eight goals to Wolverhampton Wanderers in a Second Division clash at Molineux. They replied through Ray Hiron and a Les Wilson own goal. The Pompey team was: John Milkins, Roy Lunniss, Alex Wilson, Bobby Campbell, Harry Harris (Cliff Portwood), Johnny Gordon, Brian Lewis, Albert McCann, Ray Hiron, Dennis Edwards, Tony Barton.

UNLUCKY THIRTEEN

After joining Pompey in December 1980, Bobby Doyle was successful with his first 12 penalties for the club. His 13th attempt was saved by Millwall goalkeeper Paul Sansome – but Billy Rafferty followed up to score.

FIRST LEAGUE CUP GOAL

Tony Priscott scored Pompey's first goal in the Football League Cup competition. He netted in a 2-0 win at home to Coventry City on 2 November 1960.

50% MISSED

Pompey were awarded 16 penalties during their 1982/83 Third Division title-winning season, but missed half. The culprits were Bobby Doyle (2), Steve Aizlewood (2), Alan Biley, Neil Webb, Trevor Ross and Colin Sullivan.

BIGGEST POST-WAR VICTORIES

Pompey's biggest post-war victory is 7-0. On 8 January 1949, as Stockport County were dumped out of the FA Cup at Fratton Park. Peter Harris scored a hat trick; Len Phillips and Ike Clarke each netted twice for Pompey. The team was: Ernie Butler, Phil Rookes, Harry Ferrier, Jimmy Scoular, Reg Flewin, Jimmy Dickinson, Peter Harris, Bert Barlow, Ike Clarke, Len Phillips, Jack Froggatt. Eight months later, on 10 September 1949, Everton were thrashed by the same scoreline in a First Division fixture at Fratton Park. The Pompey team was: Ernie Butler, Bill Hindmarsh, Harry Ferrier, Jimmy Scoular, Reg Flewin, Jimmy Dickinson, Peter Harris, Duggie Reid, Ike Clarke, Len Phillips, Jack Froggatt. Duggie Reid grabbed a hat trick, and his fellow forwards Harris, Clarke, Phillips, and Froggatt all scored a goal apiece.

NOT EVEN A CORNER

On 5 December 1931, Newcastle United and Pompey played out a goalless draw at St. James's Park. It is believed to be the only Football League match that failed to produce a corner kick.

ABERDARE ATHLETIC

Pompey were Aberdare Athletic's first Football League opponents. The Welsh club became members of Division Three (South) in 1921 but only lasted in the league for six years. That first match was played at their Ywys Field ground in front of 9722 people on 27 August 1921, and the sides fought out a goalless draw.

FIRST LOAN PLAYER

The first player to play for Pompey on loan was York City goalkeeper Bob Widdowson, who made four appearances during the 1969/70 season. First-choice keeper John Milkins fractured a cheekbone in a 4-0 defeat at Watford on 18 October, so Ray Potter stepped up to replace him. Potter broke two fingers in only his second game – a 3-3 draw at Carlisle – and so Widdowson kept goal for the next four matches before Milkins returned from injury.

BIG CROWD

Pompey were leading the Second Division when Fratton Park's biggest league crowd outside Division One – 35,038 – saw them defeat second-placed Blackpool 3-1 on 2 December 1967. Cliff Portwood gave Pompey the lead, but Alan Skirton equalised close to half-time. Late goals by Mick Travers and Ray Pointer earned Pompey victory to leave them top, two points clear of the Seasiders, but neither side gained promotion.

THREE DIVISIONS

David Pullar played for Pompey in three divisions while still a teenager. He made his debut in Division Two as a substitute in Pompey's 2-1 win at home to Orient in April 1976, but relegation at that time was already assured. He played on the wing as Pompey spent two years in Division Three, and in August 1979 he appeared in the club's first match in the Fourth Division, six months before his 20th birthday.

YOUNGEST GOALSCORER

Pompey's youngest goalscorer is Jimmy White, who was only 16 years 291 days when he scored on his debut in a First Division home match against Birmingham City on 21 March 1959.

FA CUP FINAL GOALSCORERS

The following players have scored in FA Cup Finals for other clubs:

Mike Trebilcock (2) ....Everton 1966
Bobby Stokes ....Southampton..........................1976
Gary Stevens................Brighton and Hove Albion 1983
Teddy Sheringham ......Manchester United 1999

FOUR DIVISIONS

Goalkeeper Alan Knight is the only player to have represented Pompey in all four divisions of the Football League. He made his debut in Pompey's 1-0 win at Rotherham in Division Three on the final day of their 1977/78 relegation season, and made a handful of appearances over the next two campaigns while the club were in Division Four. He became first-choice goalkeeper as Pompey climbed up through divisions Three and Two, and completed his full set on 15 August 1987, when Pompey played their first top-flight fixture since 1959, losing 4-2 away to Oxford United.

ONE CUP FINAL MANAGER

Jack Tinn is the only manager to guide Pompey to a Cup Final. He took the team to their first FA Cup Final in 1929, but saw them lose to Bolton Wanderers; in 1934 he returned with his side to Wembley for the 2-1 defeat by Manchester City. In 1939, he finally led Pompey to FA Cup triumph, they beat Wolverhampton Wanderers 4-1 at Wembley. Tinn was also manager when Pompey lost 2-0 to Brentford in the London Wartime Cup Final.

SCORED FOR ENGLAND

The following Pompey players have scored for England, although only Jack Froggatt (2) and Mark Hateley (1) netted for their country while on the club's books:

Mike Channon	21
Paul Mariner	13
Teddy Sheringham	11
Mark Hateley	9
Peter Crouch	8
Darren Anderton	7
John Atyeo	5
Neil Webb	4
Gerry Francis	3
Paul Merson	3
Jack Froggatt	2
Ray Pointer	2
Steve Stone	2
Ray Crawford	1
Chris Lawler	1

OLDEST PROGRAMME

The Pompey programme believed to be the oldest in existence dates back to 13 February 1901 - shortly after the death of Queen Victoria. The match was a Western League fixture between Pompey and Bristol Rovers that the hosts won 3-0, with the goals coming from Bob Marshall, Frank Bedingfield and John Lewis.

BORN ON THE SAME DAY

Pompey quartet Harry Ferrier, Freddie Evans, Harry Walker and Lindy Delapenha were all born on 20 May.

HAVE A BALL

In 1939 FA Cup-winning captain Jimmy Guthrie was presented with the match ball, but he sportingly gave it to referee Tommy Thompson.

FIRST SEASON IN FOOTBALL LEAGUE

Pompey were founder members of the Football League Division Three South, and they ended the season in twelfth place. They were knocked out of the FA Cup in the third round by South Shields, who were managed by Jack Tinn, later to take charge of Pompey.

Football League Division Three (South) 1920/21

	Pl	W	D	L	F	A	W	D	L	F	A	Pts
1 Crystal Palace	42	15	4	2	45	17	9	7	5	25	17	59
2 Southampton	42	14	5	2	46	10	5	11	5	18	18	54
3 Queens Park Rangers	42	14	4	3	38	11	8	5	8	23	21	53
4 Swindon Town	42	14	5	2	51	17	7	5	9	22	32	52
5 Swansea Town	42	9	10	2	32	19	9	5	7	24	26	51
6 Watford	42	14	4	3	40	15	6	4	11	19	29	48
7 Millwall	42	11	5	5	25	8	7	6	8	17	22	47
8 Merthyr Town	42	13	5	3	46	20	2	10	9	14	29	45
9 Luton Town	42	14	6	1	51	15	2	6	13	10	41	44
10 Bristol Rovers	42	15	3	3	51	22	3	4	14	17	35	43
11 Plymouth Argyle	42	10	7	4	25	13	1	14	6	10	21	43
12 POMPEY	42	10	8	3	28	14	2	7	12	18	34	39
13 Grimsby Town	42	12	5	4	32	16	3	4	14	17	43	39
14 Northampton	42	11	4	6	32	23	4	4	13	27	52	38
15 Newport County	42	8	5	8	20	23	6	4	11	23	41	37
16 Norwich C	42	9	10	2	31	14	1	6	14	13	39	36
17 Southend U	42	13	2	6	32	20	1	6	14	12	41	36
18 Brighton	42	11	6	4	28	20	3	2	16	14	41	36
19 Exeter City	42	9	7	5	27	15	1	8	12	12	39	35
20 Reading	42	8	4	9	26	22	4	3	14	16	37	31
21 Brentford	42	7	9	5	27	23	2	3	16	15	44	30
22 Gillingham	42	6	9	6	19	24	2	3	16	15	50	28

THREE BROTHERS

The only occasion in which three brothers took part in an FA Cup semi-final was in 1934, when Pompey and Leicester City met at Highbury. Willie and Jack Smith were in the Pompey line-up, facing their younger brother Sep, who played at right-half for Leicester.

POMPEY'S HISTORICAL LEAGUE STATUS

1899-1911 ....Southern League Division One
1911-12 ....Southern League Division Two
1912-15..............................Southern League Division One
1915-16 ....South Western Combination
1916-17 ....London Combination
1917-19 ....South Hants War League
1919-20..............................Southern League Division One
1920-21..Division Three
1921-24 ....Division Three (South)
1924-27 ....Division Two
1927-39 ....Division One
1939-40 ....Regional League South 'B' and 'C'
1940-41 ....Football League South
1941-42 ....London War League
1942-46...League South
1946-59 ....Division One
1959-61 ....Division Two
1961-62..Division Three
1962-76 ....Division Two
1976-78..Division Three
1978-80 ....Division Four
1980-83..Division Three
1983-87 ....Division Two
1987-88 ....Division One
1988-92 ....Division Two
1992-2003 ....Division One
2003 to date ....FA Premier League

GOALKEEPER SCORED THE WINNER

Pompey and Northern Ireland goalkeeper Norman Uprichard was a more than useful outfield player, and had he not been such a capable custodian, could well have earned his living "out in the field." On 3 January 1959, while playing in goal for Pompey Reserves against Nottingham Forest, he injured his wrist. This was before substitutes were allowed, so Uprichard moved to outside-right…and scored the winning goal.

FRATTON GOES ALL-SEATER

During the summer of 1997, the club installed seats on the terraces to conform with the Taylor report. When the season began, only 5,000 had been installed, so the capacity of the ground was only 12,000.

LOST AND FOUND

Ernie Butler was so proud of the two First Division championship medals he won with Pompey, he would carry them in his pocket at all times, gaining great delight in showing them off to anybody who was interested. Shortly before his death in 2002, he discovered one was missing, and appeals for the medal's safe return were made in the local media. It was eventually found by a road sweeper and returned to a relieved Mr Butler.

BIGGEST FOURTH DIVISION CROWDS

Pompey's attendances were the envy of all lower division clubs while they resided in the Fourth Division between 1978 and 1980. Below is a list of the top five:

20/10/1979	Pompey 4 Bradford City 1	23,871
01/01/1980	Pompey 1 Aldershot 3	23,462
22/03/1980	Pompey 1 Walsall 2	21,785
23/10/1980	Pompey 0 Newport County 2	20,755
23/02/1980	Pompey 4 Huddersfield Town 1	19,203

A.E. KNIGHT

Arthur Egerton Knight was an England amateur international during his spell with Pompey from 1908 until 1922, and also won a cap for the full England side, against Northern Ireland in 1920. Always referred to in the press as A.E. Knight, he played for Surrey as a schoolboy, and joined Godalming after leaving school. He began working for an insurance company and, through his job, moved to Portsmouth. Pompey snapped up the left-back, and he spent a season in the reserves before making his first-team debut in Southern League Division One. He enjoyed an eventful career, winning 30 amateur international caps, and he also represented Great Britain in the 1912 Olympics in Stockholm. He captained the Pompey side that won the 1920 Southern League Championship, and but for injury would have led the side in their first Football League fixture. Knight, who played county cricket for Hampshire over a period of ten years, left Pompey in 1922, and played out the remainder of his football career with the legendary Corinthians amateur club, who granted him life membership.

TON-UP ATKINS

When Bill Atkins scored his first goal for Pompey in a 2-0 home win over Blackburn Rovers in August 1969, it was his 100th in league football.

TREBS' TREBLES

Mike Trebilcock scored two hat tricks during a five-year spell with Pompey, and they came in the same month. On 3 October 1970, he grabbed a second-half treble in a 5-0 win over Watford at Fratton Park, and four weeks later notched a hat-trick in the first 16 minutes of Pompey's 4-1 home win against Blackburn Rovers.

UP FOR THE CUP

FA Cup Final
27 April 1929, Wembley Stadium
Bolton Wanderers (0) 2   *v*   Pompey (0) 0
Butler, Blackmore
Attendance 99,570

Pompey played in their first FA Cup Final in 1929, but Bolton were making their third visit to Wembley in seven years, having won the trophy in 1923 and 1926. Pompey were forced to reshuffle their side when left-back Tommy Bell was injured close on half-time – he moved to outside-left with both legs bandaged. Billy Butler scored Bolton's first goal with 12 minutes left, then Harold Blackmore made certain with a terrific shot three minutes from time. POMPEY: Jock Gilfillan, Alex Mackie, Tommy Bell, Jimmy Nichol, John McIlwaine, Dave Thackeray, Fred Forward, Jack Smith, Johnny Weddle, Dave Watson, Freddie Cook.

FIRST £100,000 DEPARTURE

The first player to be sold by Pompey for a six-figure sum was Steve Foster, who moved to Brighton and Hove Albion for £150,000 in June 1979. A product of Pompey's youth policy, Foster began his career as a centre forward, but was converted to centre-half. At the time of his transfer, Pompey were a Fourth Division club, and his new team had recently won promotion to the First Division.

POINTER INSPIRES FIRST WIN

Pompey's first win at Burnley, in December 1971, was inspired by former Turf Moor legend Ray Pointer. Manager Ron Tindall had recalled the 35-year-old to his struggling side to "show them what spirit is all about". Pompey were not expected to get much from the Second Division clash with the high-riding Clarets, but Pointer led them to a well-deserved 3-1 victory. Also in the Pompey side were former Burnley players Fred Smith and Colin Blant.

BRAVE TILSED

Goalkeeper Ron Tilsed played the last 20 minutes of Pompey's 3-3 draw away to Luton Town in September 1973 with a broken arm. Centre-forward Ron Davies, back helping out the defence, struck Tilsed's arm while attempting to clear the ball. Tilsed, obviously in severe pain, defiantly refused to leave the field and helped Pompey to a point.

LOSING THE LEAD

All teams lose leads, but three in Pompey's history deserve a mention:

1 January 1985: Pompey were leading Fulham 4-0 at Fratton Park in Division Two, only for the Londoners to hit back after the break and draw level at 4-4 with a last-minute penalty.

5 November 1977: Pompey were leading Tranmere Rovers 2-0 at half-time in a Third Division fixture, and everything seemed to be going their way, with the visitors missing a penalty. But things changed in the second half, with Tranmere scoring five times to win the match 5-2.

3 October 1959: Pompey took a 3-0 lead after only 13 minutes of their Second Division meeting with Huddersfield Town at Leeds Road, but eventually lost the match 6-3.

GENEROUS CLIFF

A Portsmouth tailor promised to donate a suit to any player who scored in the 1939 FA Cup Final against Wolves. Cliff Parker scored twice, so he shared the value of the second suit between the two reserves, Abe Smith and Bill Bagley.

BIGGEST LEAGUE WIN

Pompey recorded their biggest Football League victory on 9 April 1927, by beating Notts County 9-1 at Fratton Park in a Second Division clash. The goalscorers were Billy Haines (3), Jerry Mackie (2), Fred Cook (2), Reg Davies and Fred Forward. The Pompey team was: Dan McPhail, George Clifford, Ted Smith, Reg Davies, Harry Foxall, Billy Moffat, Fred Forward, Jerry Mackie, Billy Haines, Dave Watson, Freddie Cook.

MET IN FOUR LEAGUES

Pompey have met three teams in all four divisions. They are Grimsby Town, Huddersfield Town, and Wimbledon.

POMPEY'S CENTENARIAN

Zillwood George (Zach) March lived to be 101 – and is believed to be the oldest ever Pompey player. He appeared three times during the 1922/23 season, following a lengthy spell with Brighton. Before he died in 1994, he was also believed to be the oldest ex-professional footballer in England at the time.

WHEN WAR BROKE OUT

When war was declared on 3 September 1939, League football was suspended, with Pompey having played three First Division fixtures. The aborted season's record was:

26/08/1939 ....Blackburn Rovers (h) 2-1
30/08/1939 ....Derby County (a)...............................0-2
02/09/1939 ....Bolton Wanderers (a) 1-2

The Pompey line-up in all three matches was: Harry Walker, Lew Morgan, Bill Rochford, Abe Smith, Tommy Rowe, Guy Wharton, Fred Worrall, Jimmy McAlinden, Jock Anderson, Bert Barlow, Cliff Parker.

PLAYED IT AT LAST

On 16 October 1946, Fratton Park staged a friendly between Pompey and Clyde, which the home side won 3-1. The match was originally arranged in 1939, but when war broke out the two clubs agreed to play it as soon as was possible. During the morning of the game, the Clyde party was received by the Lord Mayor of Portsmouth, and given a tour of HMS Victory.

WELSH CAPS

When Ron Davies and Phil Roberts played for Wales in their 2-0 defeat by England at Cardiff in May 1974, they were the first Pompey players to appear for the Welsh national side since Freddie Cook won his last cap in November 1931.

WEDDLE TOP MAN

When football was suspended due to the outbreak of war in 1939, Johnny Weddle held the club's appearance and goal-scoring record. He scored 168 League goals in 368 appearances, and added another 13 goals from 28 FA Cup games.

HIRON'S SHORTENED RETURN

Ray Hiron spent 11 years with Pompey before his transfer to Reading in 1975, so when the Royals visited Fratton Park for the first time after his move to Elm Park, he was desperate to play, even though he was suffering from a leg injury. He started the match, but was forced to limp off after only three minutes.

EUROPEAN CUP AT FRATTON PARK

The European Cup was paraded round Fratton Park in August 1982, when holders Aston Villa played Pompey in a testimonial match for Alex Cropley, a former player of both clubs.

WAS IT WORTH IT?

When Pompey faced Newcastle United at Fratton Park in October 1991, they hadn't conceded a league goal on home soil, so Magpies striker Mick Quinn promised he would be the first player to put one past his former Pompey team-mate Alan Knight. Although Pompey won the match 3-1, Quinn kept his promise, but with unfortunate consequences. When forcing the ball over the line, he collided with a post and received an injury that would keep him out of action for five months.

GEORGE BEST

George Best was arguably the greatest player ever to grace the English game, but he only played at Fratton Park on one occasion – and that was a friendly. In December 1973, Pompey drew 1-1 with Manchester United in one of two friendly matches against major sides staged to celebrate the Club's 75th anniversary. Northern Ireland international Best played the full 90 minutes. The only other match in which he faced Pompey was on 7 October 1970, when United beat Pompey 1-0 in a third round League Cup tie at Old Trafford.

CONSECUTIVE HAT TRICKS

Two Pompey players have scored hat tricks in consecutive matches. In October 1963, Ron Saunders grabbed three goals in a 5-2 win against Newcastle United at Fratton Park, then a week later netted three times at Brisbane Road as Leyton Orient were beaten 6-3. In November 1983, Mark Hateley scored three in a 5-0 home victory over Cambridge United, and four days later hit three more at Fratton Park, in the 4-0 drubbing of Grimsby Town. All the matches came in the Second Division.

WHAT A SACRIFICE

Irishman Gerry Bowler sacrificed a large amount of money to try his luck in the English game with Pompey. His wages at Fratton Park would have been no more than £10 per week, but rules in Northern Ireland were different. With his former club Distillery, he was receiving £13 per week, and a £200 signing-on fee at the beginning of each season.

THE DOOG NEVER FACED POMPEY

Northern Ireland star Derek Dougan made his Football League debut for Pompey in a 3-0 win against Manchester United at Old Trafford on 19 October 1957, and left Fratton Park in 1959. He enjoyed a long, colourful career, playing for Blackburn Rovers, Aston Villa, Peterborough United, Leicester City, and Wolverhampton Wanderers, but never once played against his first English club.

POMPEY FOR ENGLAND

The following Pompey players have represented England while with the club:

Jimmy Dickinson 48
Jack Froggatt 13
Mark Hateley..4
Len Phillips 3
Jack Smith 3
Reg Flewin*...2
Peter Harris 2
Albert Houlker 2
Fred Worrall...2
Danny Cunliffe 1
Arthur Knight 1

* appearances made during wartime

EMERGENCY GOALKEEPER

On the morning of 7 January 1933, Pompey sent a telegram to Salisbury City of the Western League requesting that Jessie Weekes, who had previously been given a trial by the Club, keep goal for them in a First Division fixture that afternoon against Sheffield United. Weekes made a hurried dash to Fratton Park, and performed heroically as the Blades were beaten 1-0. It culminated in Weekes being signed on professionally with Pompey, but he failed to make another first-team appearance.

CHARITY SHIELD

Pompey have only appeared in one Charity Shield final. As Football League champions in 1949 they played FA Cup holders Wolverhampton Wanderers at Highbury in October of that year and drew 1-1, the goal coming from Duggie Reid. The teams kept the shield for six months each. They might have appeared a year later, when they won the Championship again – but the match was played between England's first-ever World Cup Finals side, and a Canadian touring team. England won 4-2.

POMPEY LOANEES BECOME HEROES

Arguably the two most dramatic goals scored in Football League history were by players who appeared briefly on loan for Pompey. In May 1989, Arsenal were leading Liverpool 1-0 with a minute to go in the First Division championship decider. Had the result stood, the trophy would have gone to Anfield, but Michael Thomas, who made three appearances for Pompey on loan from Arsenal during the 1986/87 campaign, netted for the Gunners, meaning that they were crowned League champions. Ten years later, in May 1999, Jimmy Glass, who played in goal for Pompey on three occasions during the 1994/95 season while on loan from Crystal Palace, scored a priceless goal for Carlisle United. The Cumbrian side were drawing 1-1 at home to Plymouth Argyle on the final day of the season, and heading out of the Football League, when Glass joined the attack – and scored a last-minute winner to keep his side in Division Three and end Scarborough's 12-year league status.

FROM ROCHDALE RESERVES

In September 1979, Phil Ashworth was languishing in Rochdale's reserve side, but a little more than a month later, he'd scored four goals in two games for promotion-seeking Pompey. Manager Frank Burrows was concerned that his reserve side lacked height and power, and signed Ashworth on a free transfer to plug the gap. An injury to Jeff Hemmerman paved the way for Ashworth to make his Pompey debut, and he scored twice in a 4-3 home win over Darlington. A fortnight later, promotion rivals Bradford City visited Fratton Park, and Ashworth again scored twice as Pompey won 4-1.

BEST SINCE 1956

Pompey finished their first season in the Premiership (2003/04) in 13th place, their best league position since 1956, when they came twelfth in the First Division.

GOALIE DIDN'T TURN UP

There must have been something about Thorneycroft Woolston that Pompey goalkeeper Ernie Collins didn't like. Twice he failed to turn up to play against against them in South Hants War League fixtures, and on both occasions Bill McKay, normally an inside-forward, took his place. The first match, in January 1918, ended in a 3-0 win for Pompey, and the second, in February 1919, was a 3-3 draw.

FROM THE ARMY TO POMPEY

Twice in comparatively recent years, two men have bought themselves out of the army to gamble on a professional career at Fratton Park. In 1989, Guy Whittingham turned his back on the services to become a goalscoring sensation with Pompey, and in 1995 Lee Bradbury, also a striker, made the switch from soldier to footballer. Another coincidence was that after leaving Fratton Park, they both returned for a second spell.

JOHN DEACON

John Deacon is, at 15 years, Pompey's longest-serving chairman. A Southampton-based property developer, he became a director in December 1972, with the promise of vast sums of money to buy new players. Taking over as chairman in May 1973, he promised success would return to Fratton Park in three years, but after spending a fortune on players the club was relegated to the Third Division in 1976, and plunged into a severe financial crisis. More heartache followed, with relegation to Division Four in 1978, but the club's fortunes slowly turned, and promotion from the basement was attained in 1980, followed by the Third Division title in 1983. Mr Deacon maintained that his aim had always been to bring First Division football to Fratton Park, and his dream was fulfilled in 1987, when Pompey finished Second Division runners-up. But the team was relegated after just one year in the top flight, and with the club once again struggling financially, Mr Deacon sold out to Jim Gregory for £2m. He died in April 1995.

ALL THRO' THE NIGHT

David Coid did not have the best preparation for his Pompey debut in November 1920. He signed from Scottish club Armadale, and travelled by train from Scotland to Portsmouth through the night before the match. He managed a goal in Pompey's 3-0 victory over Southend, and looked a promising acquisition, but in his eighth Pompey outing he sustained an injury that forced his premature retirement.

HAND MANAGES HIS COUNTRY

Eoin Hand is the only former Pompey player to manage his country. The defender, who made 18 appearances for the Republic of Ireland between 1970 and 1975, managed Ireland from April 1980 until November 1985. His record was played 40, won 11, drew 9, lost 20.

PROMOTION

Pompey won the Division Three (South) championship in 1923-24. They clinched the title by beating Swindon Town 4-1 at Fratton Park in the penultimate match of the season and wound up the campaign by winning 2-0 at Gillingham, thanks to two goals by Steve Dearn, on his club debut.

Football League Division Three (South) 1923/24

	Pl	W	D	L	F	A	W	D	L	F	A	Pts
1 POMPEY	42	15	3	3	57	11	9	8	4	30	19	59
2 Plymouth Argyle	42	13	6	2	46	15	10	3	8	24	19	55
3 Millwall	42	17	3	1	45	11	5	7	9	19	27	54
4 Swansea Town	42	18	2	1	39	10	4	6	11	21	38	52
5 Brighton	42	16	4	1	56	12	5	5	11	12	25	51
6 Swindon Town	42	14	5	2	38	11	3	8	10	20	33	47
7 Luton Town	42	11	7	3	35	19	5	7	9	15	25	46
8 Northampton Town	42	14	3	4	40	15	3	8	10	24	32	45
9 Bristol Rovers	42	11	7	3	34	15	4	6	11	18	31	43
10 Newport County	42	15	4	2	39	15	2	5	14	17	49	43
11 Norwich City	42	13	5	3	45	18	3	3	15	15	41	40
12 Aberdare Athletic	42	9	9	3	35	18	3	5	13	10	40	38
13 Merthyr Town	42	11	8	2	33	19	0	8	13	12	46	38
14 Charlton Athletic	42	8	7	6	26	20	3	8	10	12	25	37
15 Gillingham	42	11	6	4	27	15	1	7	13	16	43	37
16 Exeter City	42	14	3	4	33	17	1	4	16	4	35	37
17 Brentford	42	9	8	4	33	21	5	0	16	21	50	36
18 Reading	42	12	2	7	35	20	1	7	13	16	37	35
19 Southend United	42	11	7	3	35	19	1	3	17	18	65	34
20 Watford	42	8	8	5	35	18	1	7	13	10	36	33
21 Bournemouth & BA	42	6	8	7	19	19	5	3	13	21	46	33
22 Queens Park Rangers	42	9	6	6	28	26	2	3	16	9	51	31

ONLY ONE DEPARTED

In December 1973, Pompey put 11 players on the transfer list in an effort to reduce the wage bill – only one player left: David Munks to Swindon Town.

THE CUP GOES BACK

As Pompey won the FA Cup in 1939, they held it throughout the whole of the War, and their first FA Cup tie after the hostilities ended was away to Birmingham City in the first match of a two-legged third round. Reg Flewin put through his own net in what proved to be the only goal of the game, and the second leg at Fratton Park ended goalless, meaning the cup's long stay on the south coast would soon be at an end.

TESTIMONIAL MATCHES

Since Jimmy Dickinson had a testimonial match in October 1965, Fratton Park has staged 15 benefit games. They are all listed below:

21/11/1967	Johnny Gordon/Alex Wilson	Pompey 2 Arsenal 0
25/03/1968	Johnny Gordon/Alex Wilson	Pompey 2 Stoke City 1
14/11/1968	Harry Harris	Pompey 1 Chelsea 0
05/05/1972	John Milkins	Pompey 0 Southampton 7
09/05/1973	Albert McCann	Pompey 4 West Ham 2
03/05/1974	Gordon Neave	Pompey 0 Southampton 0
06/05/1975	Ray Hiron	Pompey 2 Southampton 1
27/04/1976	Malcolm Manley	Pompey 3 Leicester City 1
18/04/1979	Eoin Hand	Pompey 2 Republic of Ireland X1 2
16/05/1980	Duggie Reid	Pompey 2 Southampton 4
14/10/1980	Steve Piper	Pompey 2 Crystal Palace 3
23/08/1982	Alex Cropley	Pompey 3 Aston Villa 4
10/05/1994	Alan Knight	Pompey 1 Southampton 5
18/05/1999	Gordon Neave	Pompey 1 West Ham 0
09/05/2000	Justin Edinburgh	Pompey 4 Tottenham Hotspur 2

CLUB BEFORE COUNTRY

Welsh international outside-left Freddie Cook put Pompey before his country in February 1928 when, after being selected for Wales, he preferred to help Pompey in their fight against relegation. Wales won their match with Northern Ireland 2-1 in Belfast, but Pompey were beaten 6-2 by Leicester City at Filbert Street.

POMPEY TRIED FOR SIR ALF

After John Mortimore was suspended as Pompey manager in September 1974, chairman John Deacon offered the job to Sir Alf Ramsey. He had been sacked by England earlier in the year, and told Mr Deacon that he was not yet ready to re-enter football management.

SOUTHEND CELEBRATE LANDMARK

Southend United celebrated their 100th match at Roots Hall on 12 March 1994 by beating Pompey 2-1. Gerry Creaney put Pompey ahead, but goals by Peter Beadle and Andy Sussex earned a win for the Essex club.

WHEN MATTHEWS PLAYED AT FRATTON

Stanley Matthews has played against Pompey at Fratton Park more than any other player. His first appearance was as a 19-year-old for Stoke City, when he scored his only goal on Pompey's ground in his side's 3-1 defeat. The results from matches he played at Fratton Park for Stoke City and Blackpool are set out below:

20/01/1934 ....Pompey 3 Stoke City 1 ....Division One
13/10/1934 ....Pompey 0 Stoke City 1 ....Division One
28/03/1936 ....Pompey 2 Stoke City 0 ....Division One
10/10/1936 ....Pompey 1 Stoke City 0 ....Division One
29/01/1938 ....Pompey 2 Stoke City 0 ....Division One
16/11/1946 ....Pompey 1 Stoke City 3 ....Division One
06/03/1948 ....Pompey 1 Blackpool 1........................Division One
13/11/1948 ....Pompey 1 Blackpool 1........................Division One
27/08/1949 ....Pompey 2 Blackpool 3........................Division One
14/10/1950 ....Pompey 2 Blackpool 0........................Division One
22/08/1951 ....Pompey 1 Blackpool 3........................Division One
23/08/1952 ....Pompey 0 Blackpool 2........................Division One
27/08/1955 ....Pompey 3 Blackpool 3........................Division One
06/04/1963 ....Pompey 0 Stoke City 3........................Division Two

TRIPLE PENALTY SAVE

On 22 September 1973, in a home match against Notts County, John Milkins saved a penalty three times – from three different players. Firstly, Kevin Randall's spot-kick was saved by Milkins, but the referee ruled that Milkins had moved. Up stepped Don Masson, and the keeper deflected his shot against the crossbar. Again, the referee decided Milkins had moved. Next Brian Stubbs took the shot, which Milkins turned over the bar.

HARRY THE LAST SURVIVOR

After Johnny Gordon and Alex Wilson retired at the end of the 1966/67 season, Harry Harris provided the last link from Pompey's First Division days. Harris went on to clock up 380 league appearances for the club before retiring in 1970.

YOUNG AWFORD

Andy Awford was Pompey's youngest player at 16 years 275 days when he played in an away game against Crystal Palace on 15 April 1989. He had by then already claimed the record for being the youngest player to play in the FA Cup competition. On 10 October 1987, he came on as substitute for Worcester City, against Boreham Wood in a qualifying round, aged 15 years 88 days.

DRESSING-ROOM RUMPUS

When the Pompey players reached the dressing-room prior to the 1942 Wartime Cup Final with Brentford, skipper Jimmy Guthrie informed manager Jack Tinn that the players would not turn out unless they were paid money they'd been owed since September 1939. All contracts had been cancelled due to the outbreak of war, and as the players were paid fortnightly they were still owed a week's money. All the directors were called to the dressing-room, and the players were told that they would never kick a ball in England again unless they went onto the field. The players held firm, and the directors reluctantly surrendered with only eight minutes left before the start of play.

SEASON'S TOP MARKSMEN

Pompey's eight highest league scorers in a season are:

Guy Whittingham (1992-93)	42
Billy Haines (1926-27)	40
Ron Saunders (1963-64)	33
Jimmy Easson (1930-31)	29
Duggie Reid (1946-47)	29
Billy Haines (1923-24)	28
Ron Saunders (1961-62)	26
Johnny Weddle (1934-35)	25

ONE FA CUP MATCH MISSED IN 18 YEARS

Jimmy Dickinson missed just one FA Cup tie in 18 years. He took part in his first FA Cup match in January 1947, when Pompey won 3-2 at Doncaster Rovers in the third round, and appeared in his 50th and last as the team lost 3-2 away to Wolverhampton Wanderers in a third round replay in January 1965. A broken ankle kept him out of the third round tie against Bristol Rovers at Eastville in 1955, which ended 2-1 to the West Country side.

TOP SCORER FOR TWO TEAMS

Colin Garwood topped Pompey's goal-scoring chart in 1979/80 – despite being sold to Aldershot midway through the campaign. He continued in goal-scoring vein at the Recreation Ground, and ended the season with a total of ten goals for the Shots, thus making him leading scorer for two different teams in the same season.

SUPERSTITIOUS WORRALL

Pompey and England outside-right Freddie Worrall must go down as the most superstitious footballer of all time. He went into every cup-tie with a small horseshoe in his pocket, a sprig of white heather pushed down each sock, and a small white elephant tied to one of his garters. He died in April 1979 – almost inevitably, on Friday 13th.

EARLY START

The earliest date on which Pompey played a Football League match is 7 August. Pompey began the 1999/2000 season on that day, and beat Sheffield United 2-0, the goalscorers being Stefani Miglioranzi and Guy Whittingham.

THE FIRST BROTHERS

Harry and Arthur Foxall were the first brothers to play together for Pompey in the Football League. Harry, first-choice centre-half throughout his four years with the club, was joined by Arthur for just one league game, which Pompey lost 5-0 at Hull City in Division Two on 24 January 1925.

FIVE AUSTRALIANS

In 1997, Terry Venables brought five Australians to the Club. Only John Aloisi was anything like successful while at Fratton Park, scoring 29 goals in 66 matches in an 18-month spell prior to a £600,000 move to Coventry City. The other four – Craig Foster, Robbie Enes, Paul Harries, and Hamilton Thorp – were all released after one season.

UNLUCKY DEBUT

Bob Cringan was a young outside-right who joined Pompey from Scottish club Parkhead in the summer of 1921. He was selected for the season's opening fixture away to Aberdare, but broke his collar-bone during the game and so didn't complete the whole match. A few months later, he returned to Scotland without featuring in the first team again.

LUCKY ESCAPE

Returning home by coach from a 1-0 defeat at Bolton Wanderers in September 1946, the Pompey party were involved in an accident at Wickham at 3.30 on Sunday morning, when the driver was unable to avoid the obstruction of an American service vehicle. Manager Jack Tinn and trainer Jimmy Stewart, who occupied the front seats, were badly bruised, but fortunately none of the players was injured.

NEUTRAL GROUNDS

Other than their Wembley appearances, Pompey have played on neutral grounds on the following occasions:

09/02/1925	Blackburn Rovers	Highbury	FAC2	0-1
18/01/1926	Derby County	Filbert Street	FAC3	0-2
23/03/1929	Aston Villa	Highbury	FAC SF	1-0
17/03/1934	Leicester City	St Andrews	FAC SF	4-1
25/03/1939	Huddersfield T	Highbury	FAC SF	2-1
19/10/1949	Wolverhampton W	Highbury	CS	1-1
26/03/1949	Leicester City	Highbury	FAC SF	1-3
08/02/1954	Scunthorpe United	Highbury	FAC4	4-0
19/03/1963	Coventry City	White Hart Lane	FAC4	1-2
19/03/1967	Hull City	Highfield Road	FAC4	1-2
05/02/1974	Orient	Selhurst Park	FAC4	2-0
05/04/1992	Liverpool	Highbury	FAC SF	1-1
13/04/1992	Liverpool	Villa Park	FAC SFR	0-0

LONG WAIT

Milan Mandaric waited five years to see Pompey win an FA Cup tie. Efforts during the first four years of his ownership ended in failure at the first hurdle, but on 3 January 2004, a last-minute goal by Yakubu Ayegbeni gave Pompey a 2-1 home win over Second Division Blackpool.

SPORTS MAIL

The Sports Mail has been an institution in the Portsmouth area for over one hundred years. Cricket, darts, snooker and bowls are just some of the sports that take their place in the paper, but chiefly the publication covers football, and Pompey in particular. First produced on 5 September 1903, the newspaper reported on Pompey's 2-1 Southern League defeat away to Reading, and has given reports on the club's Saturday matches ever since, selling many millions of copies.

TRIBUTE TO AARON FLAHAVAN

Pompey's first home match of the 2001/02 season against Bradford City was preceded by a tribute to goalkeeper Aaron Flahavan, who was killed in a car accident a fortnight earlier. There was a moving address by club chaplain Andy Rimmer before the singing of 'Abide With Me'. Flahavan's girlfriend then laid a wreath in the Fratton End goalmouth, and this was followed by a minute's silence.

GORDON NEAVE

Gordon Neave was one of Pompey's unsung heroes, working in various roles over a period of 51 years. He arrived at Fratton Park as a player in 1948, and while Pompey were winning the first of their two successive First Division titles, he played regularly at right-half for the reserve team. He was transferred to Bournemouth in 1950, and later moved to Aldershot, but returned to Fratton Park in 1959. For the next 40 years, he worked for the club variously as a coach, trainer, physiotherapist, and kit man. He was awarded a testimonial in 1974, and another when he retired in 1999.

MATCH ABANDONED

The first home match to be a victim of the weather occurred on 18 January 1908. Pompey were leading Northampton 1-0 in the Southern League when the match was abandoned because of fog. The most recent match to be abandoned at Fratton Park was a First Division clash with Aston Villa on 15 January 1955. Pompey were 2-1 down with only 11 minutes remaining when the match was abandoned because of fog, sparking a storm of protests from the visiting team. In the morning, the Fratton Park pitch had resembled a swimming pool, but a number of soldiers from Hilsea helped the Pompey groundstaff make the surface playable. The home side led at the break, thanks to a goal from Gordon Dale, but strikes by Derek Pace and Will Baxter sent Villa into the lead. As thick fog descended in the second half, there were jeers and slow hand-clapping from the crowd - at 14,587 the lowest since the war - and referee Mr. Pullen from Bristol had no alternative but to end the match.

TOP OF DIVISION TWO

Pompey went top of Division Two for the first time since being relegated from the First Division in 1959 following a 3-0 victory over Hull City at Fratton Park on 4 November 1967. Nick Jennings gave the Blues a 1-0 half-time lead, and Albert McCann struck twice in the second-half.

LADIES' DAY

It was Ladies' Day at Fratton Park when Pompey entertained Manchester City on 8 January 1966. To encourage wives and girlfriends to become Fratton regulars, they were made guests of the club in the centre section of the North Stand.

BAD START, GOOD FINISH

In 1937/38, Pompey had to wait until their 16th League match to claim their first victory, 4-0 at home to Derby County. The first 18 games brought a return of only five points, but the last 27 fixtures earned them 33, compared to the 37 won by champions Arsenal. Pompey finished in 19th place, two points above the relegated clubs.

BIGGEST LEAGUE DEFEAT

Pompey's heaviest Football League defeat occurred on 20 October 1928 at Filbert Street, where Leicester City beat them 10-0. The Pompey team was: Dan McPhail, George Clifford, Jock McColgan, Jimmy Nichol, John McIlwaine, Dave Thackeray, Fred Forward, Bobby Irvine, Johnny Weddle, Dave Watson, Freddie Cook.

PRAISE FROM CHARLTON

Pompey earned praise from Bobby Charlton after they lost to Manchester United in the third round of the League Cup at Old Trafford on 7 October 1970. Charlton, who scored the only goal of the game, said, "I thought Pompey were unlucky to lose and it was a treat to play against a team who at no time tried to kick anyone up in the air."

HUGHIE GALLACHER

Hughie Gallacher was the only player to visit Fratton Park in the First Division with four different clubs. He turned out for Newcastle United, Chelsea, Derby County, and Grimsby Town.

ANDERTON NOT FOR SCOTLAND

Darren Anderton was eligible to play for Scotland through his father, and as a Pompey apprentice he travelled north of the border to the Scottish Youth trials. He was ignored, and returned to Portsmouth determined to play for England if ever the chance arose. Following his £1.7m move to Tottenham Hotspur in 1992, he went on to gain 30 England caps.

FIRST PREMIERSHIP AWAY WIN

Pompey's first away win in the Premiership came against Blackburn Rovers on 27 March 2004. Yakubu Ayegbeni coolly side-footed home the winning goal after Teddy Sheringham had put Pompey ahead from a free-kick, only for Matt Taylor to score in his own goal for Rovers' equaliser.

DID WELL TO DRAW

Early in 1994, Pompey, as a mid-table First Division side, earned away draws with the Premiership's top two teams. On 8 January, they travelled to Ewood Park to face second-placed Blackburn Rovers in the FA Cup third round, and Alan McLoughlin scored a hat trick for the visitors in a 3-3 draw. Four days later, Paul Walsh scored both goals as Pompey held Premiership leaders Manchester United 2-2 at Old Trafford in the quarter-final of the League Cup. Unfortunately Pompey were beaten in both replays – 3-1 by Blackburn and 1-0 by United.

LIFE OF REILLY

Matt Reilly was the regular goalkeeper in the Southern League for the Royal Artillery team, and with their demise in 1898, he became Pompey's first goalkeeper. He was capped twice for Ireland, and helped Pompey win the Southern League championship in 1901/02. He was responsible for an alteration in the laws of the game. At Donnybrook in his youth, he played gaelic football, and his habit of bouncing the ball as he dodged opponents caused the Football Association to prohibit the handling of the ball by goalkeepers outside the penalty area.

DRAMATIC FINISH

Two goals in the last two minutes earned Pompey a 5-3 victory at Walsall in Division Two on 15 December 1962. They fell behind to a goal by Colin Taylor on 13 minutes, but stormed into a 3-1 lead through goals by Johnny Gordon, Ron Saunders, and David Dodson. Jimmy O'Neill and Taylor scored for the Saddlers to make the score 3-3, but in the dying moments Dodson netted for Pompey before Tony Barton scored with the last kick of the game.

FIRST POST-WAR INTERNATIONAL

Jimmy McAlinden was the first Pompey player to win international caps after the Second World War, making three appearances for Northern Ireland between June and September 1946.

ARSENAL GOALKEEPERS

Two Arsenal goalkeepers appeared for Pompey on loan during the 1972/73 season. Graham Horn joined on loan for a spell which was initially planned to last for the whole season, but after playing 22 league games for Pompey he was sold by the Gunners to Luton Town in February of that season. A month later Arsenal loaned out Ron Tilsed until the end of the season.

PROMOTION TO DIVISION ONE

Pompey were promoted to the First Division on 7 May 1927 thanks to a victory over Preston North End 5-1 at Fratton Park on the last day of the season. In those days of goal average rather than goal difference, it was a close run thing: Pompey pipped Manchester City by a 200th part (or 0.005) of a goal. If City had scored one more goal, or Pompey one fewer, the Sky Blues would have gone up instead. Billy Haines was Portsmouth's top scorer with 40 goals.

Football League Division Two 1926/27

	Pl	W	D	L	F	A	W	D	L	F	A	Pts
1 Middlesbrough	42	18	2	1	78	23	9	6	6	44	37	62
2 POMPEY	42	14	4	3	58	17	9	4	8	29	32	54
3 Manchester City	42	15	3	3	65	23	7	7	7	43	38	54
4 Chelsea	42	13	7	1	40	17	7	5	9	22	35	52
5 Nottingham Forest	42	14	6	1	57	23	4	8	9	23	32	50
6 Preston North End	42	14	4	3	54	29	6	5	10	20	43	49
7 Hull City	42	13	4	4	43	19	7	3	11	20	33	47
8 Port Vale	42	11	6	4	50	26	5	7	9	38	52	45
9 Blackpool	42	13	5	3	65	26	5	3	13	30	54	44
10 Oldham Athletic	42	12	3	6	50	37	7	3	11	24	47	44
11 Barnsley	42	13	5	3	56	23	4	4	13	32	64	43
12 Swansea Town	42	13	5	3	44	21	3	6	12	24	51	43
13 Southampton	42	9	8	4	35	22	6	4	11	25	40	42
14 Reading	42	14	1	6	47	20	2	7	12	17	52	40
15 Wolverhampton W	42	10	4	7	54	30	4	3	14	19	45	35
16 Notts County	42	11	4	6	45	24	4	1	16	25	72	35
17 Grimsby Town	42	6	7	8	39	39	5	5	11	35	52	34
18 Fulham	42	11	4	6	39	31	2	4	15	19	61	34
19 South Shields	42	10	8	3	49	25	1	3	17	22	71	33
20 Clapton Orient	42	9	3	9	37	35	3	4	14	23	61	31
21 Darlington	42	10	3	8	53	42	2	3	16	26	56	30
22 Bradford City	42	6	4	11	30	28	1	5	15	20	60	23

POMPEY PLAYER OF THE YEAR

There have been 32 different winners of the Pompey Player of the Year
award since fans first started voting in 1968.

1967/68	Ray Pointer
1968/69	John Milkins
1969/70	Nick Jennings
1970/71	David Munks
1971/72	Richard Reynolds
1972/73	Not awarded
1973/74	Paul Went
1974/75	Mick Mellows
1975/76	Paul Cahill
1976/77	Not awarded
1977/78	Not awarded
1978/79	Peter Mellor
1979/80	Joe Laidlaw
1980/81	Keith Viney
1981/82	Alan Knight
1982/83	Alan Biley
1983/84	Mark Hateley
1984/85	Neil Webb
1985/86	Noel Blake
1986/87	Noel Blake
1987/88	Barry Horne
1988/89	Mick Quinn
1989/90	Guy Whittingham
1990/91	Martin Kuhl
1991/92	Darren Anderton
1992/93	Paul Walsh
1993/94	Kit Symons
1994/95	Alan Knight
1995/96	Alan Knight
1996/97	Lee Bradbury
1997/98	Andy Awford
1998/99	Steve Claridge
1999/00	Steve Claridge
2000/01	Scott Hiley
2001/02	Lewis Buxton
2002/03	Svetoslav Todorov
2003/04	Linvoy Primus
2004/05	Dejan Stefanovic
2005/06	Gary O'Neil

NEW MILLENNIUM

Pompey's first match of the new Millennium was a First Division clash away to Norwich City, which ended in a 2-1 defeat. Pompey's scorer was Lee Bradbury.

CHRISTMAS DAY

Time was when Christmas Day was part of the Football League calendar, but Pompey have not been in action on 25 December since they were beaten 7-4 by Chelsea at Stamford Bridge in 1957. Pompey's Football League results from matches played on Christmas Day are:

1920 ..Watford 3 Pompey 2 ....Division Three (South)
1922 ..Brighton 7 Pompey 1 ......Division Three (South)
1923 ..Millwall 2 Pompey 0 ....Division Three (South)
1924 ..Pompey 0 Crystal Palace 0 ....Division Two
1925 ..Stockport County 3 Pompey 3 ....Division Two
1926 ..Pompey 0 Nottingham Forest 0 ......Division Two
1928 ..Pompey 3 Aston Villa 2 ....Division One
1929 ..Pompey 0 Arsenal 1 ....Division One
1930 ..West Ham 4 Pompey 3......................Division One
1933 ..Liverpool 3 Pompey 3 ....Division One
1934 ..Blackburn Rovers 0 Pompey 0 ....Division One
1935 ..Pompey 3 Derby County 0 ....Division One
1936 ..Charlton Athletic 0 Pompey 0..........Division One
1937 ..Pompey 3 Preston North End 2 ......Division One
1946 ..Pompey 0 Arsenal 2 ....Division One
1947 ..Manchester United 3 Pompey 2 ....Division One
1948 ..Chelsea 1 Pompey 2..........................Division One
1950 ..Pompey 1 Chelsea 3..........................Division One
1951 ..Arsenal 4 Pompey 1 ....Division One
1953 ..Tottenham Hotspur 1 Pompey 1 ....Division One
1954 ..Blackpool 2 Pompey 2 ....Division One
1957 ..Chelsea 7 Pompey 4..........................Division One

COUSINS PLAYING FOR ENGLAND

Jack Froggatt and his cousin, Redfern Froggatt of Sheffield Wednesday, played together in the same England side. In November 1952, they were in the team that beat Belgium 5-0 at Wembley, and in April 1953 both appeared in a 2-2 draw with Scotland, also at Wembley. Their third and last match together for the national side came in June 1953 in New York, where England beat the USA 6-3.

FIRST IN THE FIRST

Freddie Cook scored Pompey's first goal in the First Division after five minutes of the 3-3 draw at Sunderland on 27 August 1927. Four days later, Fratton Park staged its first Division One match, and Cook gave his team an early lead in the 3-1 victory over Aston Villa.

THE TRAINER TREATED HIMSELF

In October 1946, Pompey were drawing 1-1 at Aston Villa when, with eight minutes to go, Pompey inside-forward Bert Barlow went down injured. Trainer Jimmy Stewart grabbed his bucket and sponge, but collapsed with a twisted knee after running onto the pitch. Duggie Reid carried Stewart to treat Barlow, who admitted he was not injured at all but was just playing for time. The trainer was then carried off the field to treat himself. Afterwards, he was advised to do no more running, so in order to retain his services, the directors appointed him Training Supervisor, and promoted reserve team trainer Jimmy Easson to the senior team.

A MIRACLE HAPPENED

On the day Pompey beat Wolverhampton Wanderers in the 1939 FA Cup Final, Mr. Will Harmer lay, as he had for over a year, stiff in bed suffering from rheumatism. With the help of his wife and mother-in-law, he struggled downstairs to hear the match commentary on the wireless. When Pompey scored their first goal, Mr Harmer jumped out of his chair, and by the time Cliff Parker grabbed the third, he could walk without any assistance. After that day, Mr Harmer was able to return to work, and although he required a stick to help him walk, he maintained that Pompey's triumph put him back on his feet and gave him the determination to get really well again.

ALOISI GOAL – THE FIRST OF THE SEASON

John Aloisi was the first player to score in the 1997/98 season when he struck after five minutes into his Pompey debut away to Manchester City. The final score was 2-2.

FIVE-MINUTE HAT TRICK

In February 1981, Mick Tait scored a hat trick in five minutes. With Pompey leading Exeter City 1-0 in a Third Division home clash at Fratton Park, Tait fired home two shots from outside the box, then completed his hat-trick with a header. Pompey won the match 5-0.

FIRST VISIT TO ANFIELD

Pompey's first visit to Anfield, in October 1927, could hardly have turned out worse. Goalkeeper Dan McPhail was declared unfit, so John Jarvie was called up for only his second first-team game. He conceded two goals in the first six minutes, and by half-time Pompey were 6-0 down. They hit back with two goals in the second half, but the home side added two more to make the final score Liverpool 8 Pompey 2.

POMPEY v EVERTON

Pompey enjoyed a run of nine successive home wins over Everton from 1946/47 to 1957/58. The Toffees were relegated from the First Division in 1951, and up to that time Pompey had beaten them at Fratton Park on five consecutive occasions since the war. After Everton's return to the top flight in 1954, Pompey won the next four Fratton duels, until in April 1959 the visitors triumphed 3-2. Since then, Everton have won all four league battles the two sides have fought out at Fratton Park.

FOUR POINTS FROM FORTY-EIGHT

After Burnley were beaten 4-2 in Division One at Fratton Park on 22 November 1959, Pompey only picked up one point at home during the rest of the season. They managed to scrape three draws away to bring their points tally to four from 24 matches. Needless to say, they were relegated.

HAPPY BIRTHDAY ALAN

Alan Ball took charge of Pompey for the first time on his 39th birthday. Pompey were playing hosts to Swansea City in Division Two, and Ball was in temporary charge following the recent sacking of Bobby Campbell. The final score was 5-0 to Pompey, and Ball was soon handed the manager's position on a permanent basis.

PLAYERS MISSED THEIR BONUS

At the beginning of the 1970/71 campaign, the Pompey players were promised a bonus of £500 per man the moment the team reached the 35-point mark. This points tally was expected to be acquired long before the end of the season, but with one match remaining the side was on 34. Pompey's opponents on the last day were Leicester City, and they won 2-1 at Fratton Park, meaning that the players missed out on their bonus.

WE WANT SATURDAYS

After Pompey's home match against Middlesbrough, scheduled for Saturday 26 March 1966, was brought forward to Friday evening to avoid clashing with the Grand National, it brought an angry response from the supporters. One season-ticket holder even asked for his money back. The Friday night crowd of 10,640 was rather disappointing, but secretary Reg Mulcock said that he feared that had the match been played on the Saturday, the gate may have dropped to 6,000. Friday evening or not, the fans saw Pompey win the Second Division clash 4-1.

EVENTFUL START FOR SVENSSON

Matthias Svensson had an eventful start to his Pompey career. He struck two goals on his full debut as Pompey beat Huddersfield Town 3-1, and in the following game was sent off in a goalless draw at Reading.

CONSECUTIVE RUN FOR SANDY KANE

Goalkeeper Sandy Kane played 104 league and cup matches for Pompey – all consecutive. He made his debut on the opening day of the 1923/24 campaign, and didn't miss a game before playing his last match for the club in a 5-1 defeat away to South Shields in October 1925.

A GOAL FOR BOTH SIDES

In February 1978, Pompey drew 1-1 at home to Exeter City in a Third Division tussle. In the second half, Pompey defender Paul Cahill gave the visitors the lead by heading into his own net, but then scored in the opposite end to atone for his mistake.

BAD START FOR YOSHI

Goalkeeper Yoshikatsu Kawaguchi had a bad start to his Pompey career, conceding a goal after only 26 seconds of his debut in a First Division clash away to Sheffield Wednesday on 3 November 2001. At least he finished up on the winning side, as Pompey won 3-2.

NAMED AFTER LINDBERGH

Lindy Delapenha made eight appearances for Pompey before moving to Middlesbrough in April 1950. His full name was Lloyd Lindbergh Delapenha, and he was born in Kingston, Jamaica on 20 May 1927, the day Charles Lindbergh flew the Atlantic – hence his middle name.

POMPEY APPEAL

The famous Pompey SOS Appeal was not the first fund to be set up to help the club. In 1960, George Turner, a vice-president of Pompey Supporters' Club, started an appeal to raise money to help the team, at the time struggling near the bottom of Division Two.

SOMETHING TO CROWE ABOUT

The introduction of substitute Jason Crowe at Selhurst Park on 17 August 2002 inspired one of Pompey's greatest ever comebacks. Losing 2-0 to Crystal Palace in the third match of the First Division promotion campaign when Crowe entered the action, Hayden Foxe headed a goal back. Within 60 seconds Crowe equalised, and three minutes later he scored what proved to be the winning goal.

WHEN POMPEY UPSET THE HAMPSHIRE FA

In 1976, Pompey's pre-season matches all took place in a Kent Cup competition. This upset the Hampshire FA, because they had not asked permission to play in it.

CYCLED ALL THE WAY

17-year-old Tom Davies cycled from Norwich to Fratton Park to watch the 1-1 draw between Pompey and Norwich City in the FA Cup third round on 7 January 1950. He was given a free ticket by a Norwich director, and after the match arrangements were made to send his bicycle back to East Anglia on the train while the young fan travelled back on the team coach.

THE FRATTON PARK PITCH

When the Fratton Park pitch was originally laid out, the measurements were 116 yards by 77 yards. The width was reduced to 73 yards in 1925, due to the erection of the South Stand, and in 1997, when work commenced on the building of the stand behind the Fratton goal, six yards were taken off the length.

TWO PENALTIES AGAINST WILSON

On 25 August 1956, Pompey full-back Alex Wilson conceded two penalties in the first three minutes of a reserve match at Leyton Orient. Don Rossiter scored from both, but his second was ordered to be retaken, and his shot hit the post before being cleared. Leyton Orient won the match 4-1.

FIRST AT THE CITY OF MANCHESTER STADIUM

Pompey were the visitors when Manchester City played their first league fixture at the City of Manchester Stadium. Playing their first away fixture in the Premiership, Pompey went ahead through Yakubu Ayegbeni on 24 minutes, and looked to have wrecked the party. But with only five seconds of normal time remaining, David Sommeil headed an equaliser for City.

SCORED FOR WALES

The following Pompey players have scored for Wales:

Ron Davies 8

Barry Horne 2

Kit Symons 2

Phil Roberts..1

HOW MARCEL GAILLARD CAME TO POMPEY

Marcel Gaillard was a Belgian outside-left who played for Pompey between 1951 and 1953. He was just 13 when the Nazis invaded Belgium, and, gathering as many belongings as they could, he and his mother and father walked to Normandy from their home in Charleroi. Their biggest fear was being separated and sent into Nazi Labour camps, but they managed to reach Normandy and boarded a train to Paris. The authorities then took charge, and they were directed to Cherbourg, where they were put on a British ship and taken to England. Eventually they embarked at Weymouth, and after a screening process for suspected fifth columnists, they were sent to Barnes, London. He signed for Crystal Palace, and was playing for their reserve side at Fratton Park when he came to the notice of Ike Clarke, who was playing for Pompey's second string that day. Clarke was so impressed that he took it upon himself to watch Gaillard again, and he strongly recommended that Pompey sign him – which they did, in February 1951. He made his debut in a 6-3 home win over Everton, and made 65 appearances for the club.

GREAT WIN WAS NEARLY CALLED OFF

Pompey's 6-1 Premiership win at home to Leeds United on 8 November 2003 was the Yorkshire club's heaviest defeat since 1959. There was a strong fear that the game might not go ahead after an electrical failure at Fratton Park. The match had already been put back ten minutes, following traffic congestion, when the floodlights failed. Eventually power was restored at 3.20pm, and the game kicked off half an hour late.

WHEN POMPEY DROPPED THE CUP

After Pompey won the FA Cup in 1939, a celebration dinner was held in Kimbells Ballroom, Osborne Road, Southsea. At some time during the evening, the lid of the trophy was knocked to the floor, and the knob was broken off. An employee at Portsmouth Gas Company was asked to weld the displaced knob back into position, and he was requested to work under complete secrecy so as not to cause any embarrassment to the club. He was rewarded with a free pint.

DUGGIE THE BRAVE

Duggie Reid was one of the bravest players to wear the Pompey shirt. On many occasions blood would be pouring from his forehead, and yet he would continually be in the thick of the action, still heading the ball. On 26 September 1953, he cracked a rib during a First Division encounter against Manchester City at Maine Road, and moved out to the wing… but he still scored the opening goal.

HIGH-SCORING DRAWS

Pompey have been involved in many high-scoring draws, the biggest being 5-5 away to Oxford United in November 1992. They were leading 5-3 with only a minute to go when Oxford struck twice. Below is a list of Football League matches that ended 4-4:

23/02/1929	Bolton Wanderers (h)	Division One
07/09/1932	Chelsea (a)	Division One
11/03/1939	Liverpool (a)	Division One
14/12/1946	Preston North End (h)	Division One
16/09/1953	Blackpool (h)	Division One
31/12/1955	Chelsea (h)	Division One
21/02/1959	Tottenham Hotspur (a)	Division One
01/01/1985	Fulham (h)	Division Two
02/02/2002	Barnsley (h)	Division One

PALMER IS SENT OFF TWICE

Carlton Palmer was the first opposition player to be sent off at Fratton Park for two different teams. On 3 December 1988, while playing for West Bromwich Albion in a goalless draw, he was ordered off for retaliating against Barry Horne, and then on 6 April 1991 he was sent off for protesting about a foul that gave Pompey a penalty against Sheffield Wednesday. Pompey won the game 2-0.

OUT ON LOAN

During October 2003 Pompey had ten players on loan at other clubs.

Lee Bradbury ....Derby County
Mark Burchill ....Wigan Athletic
Deon Burton ....Swindon Town
Shaun Cooper ....Leyton Orient
Kevin Harper ....Norwich City
Gary O'Neil ....Walsall
Courtney Pitt ....Luton Town
Carl Robinson ....Rotherham United
Jamie Vincent ....Walsall
Rowan Vine ....Colchester United

HIRON BEATS OWN RECORD

Ray Hiron was Pompey's top scorer in 1968-69 with 17, and the following season he had scored 15 with one fixture of the season remaining. That match was played away to Hull City, and Hiron scored all Pompey's goals in a 3-3 draw to beat his previous season's tally.

BLADES HIT FIVE – THREE TIMES

Sheffield United hit five goals against Pompey in three consecutive league matches. In August 1969, they beat Pompey 5-1 at Fratton Park, and won 5-0 in the return fixture at Bramall Lane. When the two sides met again at Fratton the following season, the Blades recorded another 5-1 victory.

THREE SIRS

After leaving Pompey in 1958, Ray Crawford played under three managers who would receive knighthoods. They were Alf Ramsey and Bobby Robson, both of whom Crawford played under at Ipswich Town, and Walter Winterbottom, who managed England when he won his two international caps.

WORKINGTON CONNECTION

In all the 26 years Workington were members of the Football League, they never met Pompey in any competition. The only transfer to take place between the two clubs occurred in June 1959, when Pompey reserve wing-half Colin Keir moved to Borough Park. He made four League appearances for the Reds.

WE ARE THE CHAMPIONS

In season 1948/49, Pompey celebrated their Golden Jubilee year by winning the League Championship. They twice broke the Fratton Park attendance record in FA Cup games, and remained unbeaten at home. The title was clinched on 23 April 1949, when Bolton Wanderers were beaten 2-1 at Burnden Park. Peter Harris and Duggie Reid were the goalscorers.

Football League Division Two 1948/49

	Pl	W	D	L	F	A	W	D	L	F	A	Pts
1 POMPEY	42	8	3	0	52	12	7	5	9	32	30	58
2 Manchester United	42	11	7	3	40	20	10	4	7	37	24	53
3 Derby County	42	17	2	2	48	22	5	7	9	26	33	53
4 Newcastle United	42	12	5	4	35	29	8	7	6	35	27	52
5 Arsenal	42	13	5	3	51	18	5	8	8	23	26	49
6 Wolverhampton W	42	13	5	3	48	19	4	7	10	31	47	46
7 Manchester City	42	10	8	3	28	21	5	7	9	19	30	45
8 Sunderland	42	8	10	3	27	19	5	7	9	22	39	43
9 Charlton Athletic	42	10	5	6	38	31	5	7	9	25	36	42
10 Aston Villa	42	10	6	5	40	36	6	4	11	20	40	42
11 Stoke City	42	14	3	4	43	24	2	6	13	23	44	41
12 Liverpool	42	5	10	6	25	18	8	4	9	28	25	40
13 Chelsea	42	10	6	5	43	27	2	8	11	26	41	38
14 Bolton Wanderers	42	10	4	7	43	32	4	6	11	16	36	38
15 Burnley	42	10	6	5	27	19	2	8	11	16	31	38
16 Blackpool	42	8	8	5	24	25	3	8	10	30	42	38
17 Birmingham City	42	9	7	5	19	10	2	8	11	17	28	38
18 Everton	42	12	5	4	33	25	1	6	14	8	38	37
19 Middlesbrough	42	10	6	5	37	23	1	6	14	9	34	34
20 Huddersfield Town	42	6	7	8	19	24	6	3	12	21	45	34
21 Preston North End	42	8	6	7	36	36	3	5	13	26	39	33
22 Sheffield U	42	8	9	4	32	25	3	2	16	25	53	33

THE END FOR COOK

Freddie Cook's magnificent Pompey career came to an unfortunate and abrupt end. The Welsh international outside-left collapsed with a twisted knee after taking a corner-kick in a home match against Chelsea in 1932.

TOP FLIGHT ONLY

Arsenal and Everton are the only two clubs that Pompey have faced in the league, in no other division than the top flight.

TAKE UP GOLF !

In 1951, the club staff encouraged the Pompey players to take up golf, and two directors, Jack Sparshatt and Guy Spriggins, donated a cup that would be competed for every season by the players on a handicap. Chairman Vernon Stokes, a former captain of the Portsmouth Golf Club, appealed to all his golfing friends to send to Fratton Park any golfing equipment they no longer required.

KEMP GOAL FOR DERBY

In October 1977, Pompey's David Kemp was the Third Division's leading goalscorer and was attracting the attention of many First Division clubs. He guested for Derby County at the Baseball Ground against Belgian champions Bruges in Roy McFarland's testimonial match so that Rams' boss Tommy Docherty could decide whether to make a bid for him. Despite scoring the second goal in Derby's 2-0 win, he remained at Fratton Park until the transfer deadline in March 1978, when he moved to another Third Division club, Carlisle United.

BERGER DELIGHT

On 18 October 2003, Pompey met Liverpool for the first time in the Premiership, and they defeated the Reds 1-0. Patrik Berger, who had recently made the move from Anfield, scored the only goal of the game in the fourth minute. This was the first time Pompey had beaten Liverpool since 12 March 1960.

LOW ATTENDANCES

The lowest attendance for a first-team match at Fratton Park was when Pompey beat Liverpool 2-1 on 25 February 1933. Only 4,031 attended the re-arranged First Division fixture on a Tuesday afternoon. The lowest post-war crowd – 4,688 – watched Pompey and Middlesbrough fight out a goalless draw in Division Two on 16 December 1972.

CLOCK TOWER

In 1905, Pompey chairman Sir John Brickwood paid for a clock tower to be built as the club spent money on ground improvements for the first time. As part of the facelift, a pavilion was built at the Frogmore Road entrance to the ground and the clock tower was added thanks to Sir John's personal donation. It only lasted 20 years because, in 1925, the new South Stand was erected, and this necessitated the tower's removal.

POMPEY PLAYERS WHO BECAME MANAGERS

Jimmy Allen	Colchester United	1948-53
Martin Allen	Brentford	2004-06
	MK Dons	2006-
Tony Barton	Aston Villa	1982-84
	Northampton Town	1984-85
Noel Blake	Exeter City	2000-01
Allan Brown	Luton Town	1966-68
	Torquay United	1969-71
	Nottingham Forest	1973-75
Bobby Campbell	Fulham	1976-80
	Portsmouth	1982-84
	Chelsea	1988-91
Tommy Casey	Grimsby Town	1975-76
Arthur Chadwick	Exeter City	1910-22
	Reading	1923-25
	Southampton	1925-31
Steve Claridge	Portsmouth	2000-01
	Millwall	2005
Jimmy Dickinson	Portsmouth	1977-79
Reg Flewin	Stockport County	1960-63
	Bournemouth	1963-65
Gerry Francis	Exeter City	1983-84
	Bristol Rovers	1987-91
	Tottenham Hotspur	1994-97
George Graham	Millwall	1982-86
	Arsenal	1986-95
	Leeds United	1996-98
	Tottenham Hotspur	1998-2000
Eoin Hand	Huddersfield Town	1988-92
Mark Hateley	Hull City	1997-98
Basil Hayward	Gillingham	1966-71
Chris Kamara	Bradford City	1995-98
	Stoke City	1998
Jack Mansell	Rotherham United	1965-67
	Reading	1969-71
Paul Merson	Walsall	2004-06
Richard Money	Scunthorpe United	1993-94
	Walsall	2006-
Ron Saunders	Oxford United	1969
	Norwich City	1969-73
	Manchester City	1973-74
	Aston Villa	1974-82

Ron Saunders (cont)	Birmingham City	1982-86
	West Bromwich Albion	1986-87
Jimmy Scoular	Bradford Park Avenue	1961-63
	Cardiff City	1964-73
	Newport County	1974-78
Malcolm Shotton	Oxford United	1998-99
Jack Surtees	Darlington	1942
Kenny Swain	Wigan Athletic	1993-94
	Grimsby Town	1997
Scot Symon	Preston North End	1953-54
Mick Tait	Hartlepool United	1996-99
Bill Thompson	Exeter City	1957-58
Ron Tindall	Portsmouth	1970-73
Paul Went	Leyton Orient	1981
Steve Wigley	Southampton	2004

PRESIDENT DICKINSON

In 1965, the year Jimmy Dickinson ended his playing career, he was made president of his hometown team Alton Town.

IT COULD ONLY GET BETTER

Harry Redknapp began his first term as manager in 2002, and got off to a miserable start. Pompey were beaten 2-0 at Preston North End, and Svetoslav Todorov was sent off in only his second match for the club.

THE FIRST NAME

Pompey was the first club to have its name printed on the front cover of the United Review, the Manchester United matchday programme. The programme was for a First Division fixture at Old Trafford on 21 October 1951, and the match ended goalless.

THIRD TIME LUCKY

It was third time lucky for George Smith when he signed Bobby Kellard for Pompey in March 1966. He first tried to sign the player when he was a teenager at Southend United, but felt the price was too high, and Kellard moved to Crystal Palace instead. Smith tried for Kellard again the following November, and agreed to pay Palace £15,000, but this time Ipswich Town won the race for his signature. When Smith heard that Kellard was not too happy at Portman Road, he contacted Ipswich boss Bill McGarry, a £15,000 deal was struck, and the Pompey manager at last got his man.

BILL PROBERT

Bill Probert was the automatic choice for the right-back berth in the club's early Football League days. Joining the club in 1911 as a 16-year-old, he made his debut away to Southampton in September 1913. He played regularly during World War I, while employed at Portsmouth Dockyard, and featured in every match of the 1919/20 season when Pompey won the Southern League championship. He was also ever-present throughout the subsequent campaign in Division Three, and continued to be a regular in the side over the next few years, only missing matches through illness or injury, and winning a Third Division championship medal in 1923/24. Midway through the 1924/25 season he was transferred to Fulham, and after his retirement from football he became licensee of the Milton Arms, close to Fratton Park. Sadly, he committed suicide on 31 August 1948.

MRS DEACON

So far, Portsmouth Football Club have only had one lady director. Mrs Joan Deacon, wife of chairman John, joined the board on 17 December 1982, and left the club in May 1988, when her husband sold out to Jim Gregory.

QUINN NOT WANTED

In January 1995, manager Jim Smith agreed to bring striker Mick Quinn back to Fratton Park on loan from Coventry City. Later in the day he was sacked, and his replacement Terry Fenwick was not interested in Quinn making a return.

CARRIED OFF ON DEBUT

17-year-old Micky Ross made his debut as a substitute on 25 February 1989 in a 1-0 defeat away to Bournemouth in Division Two. He replaced the injured Terry Connor, but was only on the field for 20 minutes before he collided with Cherries' Shaun Teale, and was carried off with a dislocated shoulder. The injury kept him out of the reckoning for six weeks.

SCORED FOR NORTHERN IRELAND

The following Pompey players have scored for Northern Ireland:

Colin Clarke	13
Derek Dougan	8
Tommy Casey	8
Ian Stewart	2

POMPEY/SOUTHAMPTON

A number of players have turned out for both Pompey and local rivals Southampton. Below are two team line ups of players who have played for both clubs.

FOOTBALL'S IN THE FAMILY

One of Pompey's greatest players, Jack Froggatt, was a member of a fine footballing family. His uncle, Frank Froggatt, played centre-half for Sheffield Wednesday, and played a key role when the Yorkshire club walked away with the Second Division title in 1925/26. He subsequently played in the Football League for Notts County and Chesterfield. Frank's son Redfern became one of the greatest players in Wednesday history, making 458 league and cup appearances at inside-forward and scoring 148 goals between 1946 and 1960. Jack's great-niece Laura now plays for Portsmouth Ladies, and she has travelled with the England party.

WHERE'S MY MONEY?

The most embarrassing of the club's debts, if by no means the biggest, when the SOS appeal was launched in 1976 was money owed to former player Albert McCann. His testimonial match against West Ham at Fratton Park in May 1973 attracted a crowd of 22,000, but three years later McCann was owed the balance – over £2,000 plus interest – of his testimonial fund of £10,300.

UNITED'S YOUNGEST PLAYER

The youngest player to appear in Manchester United's first team is Jeff Whitefoot, who made his debut aged 16 years 105 days against Pompey at Old Trafford on 15 April 1950. It was a curious decision by Matt Busby to select the youngster, considering the importance of the match. Before the game, United led the First Division with 48 points from 39 matches, while Pompey were lying third, having collected 47 points from 38 matches. Late goals by Duggie Reid and Jack Froggatt gave Pompey a 2-0 victory, and they went top of the table while United dropped to third. When the season ended three weeks later, Pompey were crowned champions, and Manchester United finished runners-up.

HORNE GOALS SPELL VICTORIES

Barry Horne scored three goals during the 1987/88 campaign, and they all came in the three victories that the team achieved on their travels. On 28 November, he scored the only goal as Pompey beat Norwich City 1-0, he grabbed the first goal in a 2-0 win at Southampton on 3 January, and then on 2 April scored in a 1-0 victory at Tottenham Hotspur.

HIGH FIVES

The last time Pompey scored five goals in the first-half was at home to Swindon Town on 19 September 1964. They led 5-0 at the break after John McClelland and Cliff Portwood scored two each with the other goal coming from Albert McCann. There was no further scoring in the second half. Ironically, Pompey had failed to score in their previous three matches.

MRS WORRALL'S DREAM

A few nights before the 1939 FA Cup Final, Mrs Worrall, wife of outside-right Fred, dreamt Pompey beat Wolverhampton Wanderers 2-0. The result was 4-1 to Pompey and they led 2-0 at the interval. Worrall joked that his wife must have woken up at half-time.

A CENTURY AT LAST

Johnny Gordon scored his 99th goal for the club in a 2-2 draw at home to Grimsby Town in Division Two on 4 April 1964, then had to wait over eight months to hit his 100th. He completed his century of goals on 19 December 1964, when he scored Pompey's second in a 3-3 draw away to Charlton Athletic, again in a Second Division fixture.

HAPPY RETURN FOR SHOWERS

On 8 September 1979, Derek Showers sustained a knee injury that seriously threatened his career during Pompey's 1-0 home win over Stockport County in a Fourth Division clash. He didn't play again all season, but was named as substitute for the first four matches of the 1980/81 campaign without getting on the pitch. In a Third Division home fixture with Rotherham United, he came on for the second-half and headed Pompey into a 2-1 lead. They eventually won the game 3-1. The following week, in a 2-0 victory at Blackpool, Showers celebrated his first start in almost a year with another goal.

OFF TO A BAD START

Pompey's worst result from their first match was on 31 August 1929, when they lost 4-0 to reigning League Champions Sheffield Wednesday at Fratton Park. They never looked like salvaging anything from the game once Ellis Rimmer had put Wednesday ahead after only three minutes.

TWO-GOAL FAREWELL

In his last match for the club, Ray Hiron scored twice as Pompey beat Southampton 2-1 at Fratton Park in his testimonial on 6 May 1975. The first goal was a header after only 35 seconds.

CONTINENTAL TOUR

Following their League Championship success in 1948/49, Pompey toured Sweden and Denmark and were unbeaten in five matches. The results and scorers were:

Denmark	2-2	(Parker, Reid),
Copenhagen XI	2-0	(Reid, Clarke),
Gothenberg Allianson	4-2	(Reid, Clarke, Phillips, Froggatt)
Aarhus	3-0	(Harris, Clarke, Barlow)
Copenhagen	3-1	(Phillips 2, Clarke)

HIGHEST POSITION

Pompey's highest league position since back-to-back championship successes in 1948/49 and 1949/50 is third in Division One. Achieved in the 1954/55 season, Pompey still had a chance of claiming their third title when Chelsea visited Fratton Park on 16 April 1955. The most exciting match of the campaign, watched by a crowd of 40,230, finished 0-0, and Chelsea went on to clinch their first League Championship.

ENGLAND PLAYERS AT THE HELM

No fewer than five Pompey managers have won caps for England:

Alan Ball 72
Jimmy Dickinson 48
Terry Fenwick 20
Graham Rix 17
John Gregory 6

P IS FOR POMPEY

Bill Davis was the Commercial Manager at Fratton Park before becoming secretary in 1977. He was such a fanatical Pompey supporter that the names of his four sons – Paul, Peter, Philip and Perry – all began with the letter P.

WRIT COULD HAVE KILLED OFF HEREFORD

Pompey issued Hereford United with a writ in May 1982, as they owed Pompey £27,000 18 months after Derek Showers and Joe Laidlaw moved to Edgar Street. Pompey were willing to take defender Chris Price to liquidate the debt, but Hereford would not agree. The money was eventually paid, and Price became a Pompey player 11 years later.

THE MORTIMORE BROTHERS

John Mortimore managed Pompey from July 1973 to September 1974. His brother Charlie made one appearance for the club as an amateur, on 25th December 1953, in a 1-1 draw with Tottenham Hotspur at White Hart Lane.

TWO RECORDS

George Smith set two records when he was transferred from Pompey to Middlesbrough in January 1969. The fee of £50,000 was the highest Middlesbrough had paid, and was also the highest Pompey had received.

LAST DAY ESCAPE

24 April 1965, Division Two: ....Northampton Town 1 Pompey 1

This vital match was played on a Saturday evening, and Pompey knew that a point would see them safe. Northampton Town were already promoted, and were unbeaten at home, so it would be no easy task. The match was also the last of Jimmy Dickinson's magnificent career, and he was applauded onto the pitch by both teams on what was his 40th birthday. Pompey started well, and Dennis Edwards, Cliff Portwood and John McClelland all had chances to put them ahead. In the 77th minute, a free-kick was lobbed into the Pompey goalmouth, and Johnny Gordon headed past his own goalkeeper John Armstrong. Pompey piled forward, and got their reward when Harry Harris headed on John McClelland's corner, allowing Alex Wilson to slam the ball home from ten yards and secure survival. POMPEY: John Armstrong, Alex Wilson, Ron Tindall, Johnny Gordon, Jimmy Dickinson, Harry Harris, John McClelland, Cliff Portwood, Dennis Edwards, Albert McCann, Tony Barton.

NICHOL AND THACKERAY

Jimmy Nichol and Dave Thackeray formed a wing-half partnership that served Pompey for eight years. Nichol was Jack Tinn's first major signing in November 1927, and Thackeray joined the club from Alloa Athletic in the summer of 1928. He was a tough competitor and played a defensive role, whereas Nichol was the more artistic, often setting up attacks. The pair played in the 1929 FA Cup Final, which Pompey lost 2-0 to Bolton Wanderers, and they returned to Wembley in 1934 to face Manchester City, finding themselves on the losing side again, as City won 2-1. Thackeray captained the side that day, having been appointed skipper in 1930. He made his final appearance in September 1935, and retired from the game at the end of that season, but Nichol was still a fixture in the side until December 1936, playing his final game for Pompey in a 5-1 home defeat by Arsenal. This was his 351st League outing in a Pompey shirt, at the time a club record. But this was not the end of their links with Pompey. Thackeray returned in 1950 to become assistant groundsman to Harold Reed, and he took charge of the 'A' team on match days. Sadly, he died in July 1954, shortly after Nichol returned to take up the position of head trainer. Tragically, in November of that year, he too died. Like Thackeray, he was only in his early 50s. A testimonial match was played in May 1955 between a Pompey XI and a team made up of former players, and the proceeds were divided between the dependants of two of the club's finest wing-halves.

WE ARE THE CHAMPIONS II

In 1949/50, Pompey won the First Division championship for the second consecutive season. A 5-1 win over Aston Villa at Fratton Park on the final day of the season meant they pipped Wolverhampton Wanderers on goal average. The average home league attendance was 37,393, while the average away league attendance was 37,797.

Football League Division One 1949-50

	Pl	W	D	L	F	A	W	D	L	F	A	Pts
1 POMPEY	42	12	7	2	44	15	10	2	9	30	23	53
2 Wolverhampton W	42	11	8	2	47	21	9	5	7	29	28	53
3 Sunderland	42	14	6	1	50	23	7	4	10	33	39	52
4 Manchester United	42	11	5	5	42	20	7	9	5	27	24	50
5 Newcastle United	42	14	4	3	49	23	5	8	8	28	32	50
6 Arsenal	42	12	4	5	48	24	7	7	7	31	31	49
7 Blackpool	42	10	8	3	29	14	7	7	7	17	21	49
8 Liverpool	42	10	7	4	37	23	7	7	7	27	31	48
9 Middlesbrough	42	14	2	5	37	18	6	5	10	22	30	47
10 Burnley	42	9	7	5	23	17	7	6	8	17	23	45
11 Derby County	42	11	5	5	46	26	6	5	10	23	35	44
12 Aston Villa	42	10	7	4	31	19	5	5	11	30	42	42
13 Chelsea	42	7	7	7	31	30	5	9	7	27	35	40
14 West Bromwich Albion	42	9	7	5	28	16	5	5	11	19	37	40
15 Huddersfield	42	11	4	6	34	22	3	5	13	18	51	37
16 Bolton Wanderers	42	10	5	6	34	22	0	9	12	11	37	34
17 Fulham	42	8	6	7	24	19	2	8	11	17	35	34
18 Everton	42	6	8	7	24	20	4	6	11	18	46	34
19 Stoke City	42	10	4	7	27	28	1	8	12	18	47	34
20 Charlton Athletic	42	7	5	9	33	35	6	1	14	20	30	32
21 Manchester City	42	7	8	6	27	24	1	5	15	9	44	29
22 Birmingham City	42	6	8	7	19	24	1	6	14	12	43	28

HOSPITAL RADIO

Pompey's 3-1 win at home to Newcastle United in Division One on 27 October 1951 was the first football match broadcast on Hospital Radio. Portsmouth Hospital Broadcasting (PHB) have not missed a home match since that day, and the service has covered many away games. On 27 October 2001, prior to Pompey's First Division home clash with Preston North End, Club director Fred Dinenage presented the radio station with a certificate on the Fratton Park pitch to mark the superb coverage they had provided for half a century.

KELLY AT SPURS

In November 1990 Mark Kelly joined Tottenham Hotspur on a month's loan. Kelly was not a regular in Pompey's struggling Second Division side, so his move to a First Division club left Pompey fans slightly puzzled. He failed to make a first-team appearance for the Londoners, but faced his Fratton team-mates in a reserve game at White Hart Lane that Tottenham Hotspur won 2-0.

POMPEY MANAGERS

1898-1901	Frank Brettell
1901-1904	Robert Blyth
1904-1911	Richard Bonney
1911-1920	Robert Brown
1920-1927	John McCartney
1927-1947	Jack Tinn
1947-1952	Bob Jackson
1952-1958	Eddie Lever
1958-1961	Freddie Cox
1961	Bill Thompson (caretaker)
1961-1970	George Smith
1970-1973	Ron Tindall
1973-1974	John Mortimore
1974	Ron Tindall (caretaker)
1974-1977	Ian St John
1977-1979	Jimmy Dickinson
1979-1982	Frank Burrows
1982-1984	Bobby Campbell
1984-1989	Alan Ball
1989-1990	John Gregory
1990-1991	Frank Burrows
1991-1995	Jim Smith
1995-1998	Terry Fenwick
1998	Keith Walden (caretaker)
1998-1999	Alan Ball
1999	Bob McNab (caretaker)
2000	Tony Pulis
2000-2001	Steve Claridge (player-manager)
2001-2002	Graham Rix
2002-2004	Harry Redknapp
2004-2005	Velimir Zajec (caretaker)
2005	Alain Perrin
2005-	Harry Redknapp

BOTH SCORERS ON LOAN

When Pompey beat Plymouth Argyle 2-0 at home in Division Two on 14 February 1976, both goal-scorers were spending a month on loan at Fratton Park. Martyn Busby of Queens Park Rangers scored the first goal, and the second came from Tony Macken, who was from Derby County.

GORDON ON SONG

Johnny Gordon possessed a fine singing voice, and in 1966 appeared on Southern Television's talent contest "Home Grown." He was pipped to first place by a singing group from Chatham.

THREE GENERATIONS

When Danny Hinshelwood made his debut for Pompey on 23 March 1996 in a goalless draw away to Crystal Palace, he was the third generation to play League football. His grandfather Wally Hinshelwood played for Fulham immediately after World War II, and went on to serve Chelsea, Reading, Bristol City, Millwall, and Newport County. His sons Martin and Paul both played for Crystal Palace during the 1970s, and Martin became manager of Pompey's youth and reserve teams in the 1990s.

WHARTON OK FOR THE CUP FINAL

On 1 April 1939, four weeks before Pompey were due to meet Wolverhampton Wanderers in the FA Cup Final, Guy Wharton was sent off in a 2-0 defeat against Birmingham City at Fratton Park. As was always the case for a sending-off in those days, the player had to attend an FA inquiry. At the hearing on 12 April, after listening to the evidence, the Commission decided to announce their decision at a later date, enabling Wharton to face his former club in the final.

CURRY TOO HOT FOR POMPEY

Bill Curry scored hat tricks against Pompey for three different clubs. On 11 March 1959, he netted a treble for Newcastle United, who won 5-1 at Fratton Park to push Pompey nearer to relegation from Division One. In July of that year, he was transferred to Brighton and Hove Albion and, on the third Saturday of the new season – 5 September 1959 – scored all three goals for his new club as they beat Pompey 3-1 at the Goldstone Ground in a Second Division fixture. His third hat trick against Pompey came on 10 May 1963, when he helped Derby County beat Pompey 4-0 at the Baseball Ground in another Second Division clash.

UPHILL FOR UPRICHARD ON DEBUT

Goalkeeper Norman Uprichard marked his Pompey debut with an own goal. With Pompey leading Tottenham Hotspur 2-0 on 8 November 1952, Uprichard made a save from Dennis Uphill. He failed to retain possession, and as he attempted to collect the ball as he lay on the ground, he had the misfortune to scoop it into his own net. There were no further goals in the match.

GILBERT AND SULLIVAN

Gilbert and Sullivan were Victorians, famous for writing comic operas, but Pompey had players of the same surnames on the books at the same time. Colin Sullivan was on the playing staff at Fratton Park when Billy Gilbert signed from Crystal Palace in 1984, but the pair never got to play in the same team.

SAME AGAIN

On 28 January 1976, Pompey were beaten 1-0 at home by Wrexham in Division Three, and the goal was scored by Graham Whittle at the Fratton End after 21 minutes. A year and a week later, Wrexham again visited Fratton Park for a Third Division fixture, and again beat Pompey 1-0. The goal was scored by Graham Whittle – at the Fratton End – after 20 minutes.

OFF 'N ON, OFF 'N ON

Wayne Rooney's first appearance at Fratton Park was quite memorable. It occurred in December 2004 with Rooney, then aged 18, beginning the match on the Everton substitutes' bench. After 25 minutes, he replaced the injured Steve Watson, and scored what proved to be the winning goal in the 42nd minute. In the second half, he deliberately bundled over Pompey's Steve Stone and, thinking he was sure to be sent off, walked down the tunnel – only for referee Uriah Rennie to wave him back on and issue him with a yellow card.

FAREWELL TO SEAMAN

David Seaman played the last match of his long career against Pompey at Fratton Park. Playing in a Premiership clash for Manchester City on 10 January 2004, the former England goalkeeper injured a shoulder in the 14th minute, and was replaced by Kevin Stuhr-Ellegaard. Two days later, he announced that the shoulder had been troubling him for some time, and that he would be retiring from football because of it.

LOST IN THE FOG

Full-back Willie Smith brought great amusement to his Pompey team-mates when they travelled to Filbert Street to play Leicester City in a First Division fixture on 19 December 1931. Late out of the tunnel, he found the two teams were lined up ready for kick-off in thick fog. Unable to see the faces of the players and forgetting that Pompey would be playing in red jerseys, he made his way towards the Leicester City team. Not surprisingly, the match was abandoned.

UNHAPPY VALLEY FOR POMPEY

Pompey were the visitors when Charlton Athletic played their first match at The Valley on 5 December 1992 after an absence of over seven years. The home side celebrated with a 1-0 victory over the Blues, the decisive goal coming from Colin Walsh after only seven minutes.

NEW SECRETARY REQUIRED

When goalkeeper Alan Barnett was transferred to Grimsby Town in December 1958, a new manager's secretary was required because the position was held by Barnett's wife Julie.

WHEN THE LIGHTS WENT OUT

On 12 January 1974, the second half of the Second Division clash between Pompey and Luton Town was held up for 24 minutes due to floodlight failure. Because of a power crisis, Pompey and Southampton shared the hire of a generator to power the lights, but in the 71st minute of the game, it broke down, leaving Fratton Park in semi-darkness. Referee Roger Kirkpatrick made an announcement asking the crowd to remain in their places while attempts were being made to restart the generator, and eventually Pompey chairman John Deacon ordered that the lights be plugged into the mains. Although this was, technically, a breach of the emergency lighting regulations, Mr Deacon emphasised that he ordered the switch-over in the interests of public safety. The match ended 0-0.

GREAT START FOR JIM

Jim Gregory purchased the club from John Deacon in 1988, and his ownership began with three successive Pompey victories. Shrewsbury Town were beaten 2-1 at Gay Meadow, and this was followed by a 3-0 win at home to Leicester City and a 4-0 victory at Fratton Park against Leeds United.

GOAL THAT NEVER WAS

On 22 October 1977, Pompey were beaten 6-1 in their Third Division away match at Shrewsbury Town, but were angered that the Shrews' second goal had been awarded. Brian Hornsby bent a shot goalwards, but it hit the side-netting. Pompey goalkeeper Steve Middleton placed the ball for a goal-kick, only to see Shrewsbury's Chic Bates playfully flick the ball into the net – and referee John Wrennall pointing to the centre-circle! As the Pompey players protested, home fans behind the goal tried to get the referee's attention, as they knew the ball had gone out of play – but to Pompey's anger, the goal stood.

RECORD FEE FOR STEPHEN

In November 1949, Pompey broke their transfer record by paying £15,000 to Bradford Park Avenue for Scottish international full-back Jimmy Stephen. This was, at the time, a British record fee for a full-back.

RELATIVES BEHIND THE SCENES

During the 1950s, in addition to Alan Barnett and his secretary wife Julie, there were two Pompey players who had relations working behind the scenes at Fratton Park. Mike Barnard's brother Sam was the club's physiotherapist, and Peter Harris' cousin Philip was the club secretary.

NEVER ON A SUNDAY

Phil Gunter, a Pompey defender from 1951 until 1964, was a Sunday School teacher, and in accordance with Football League regulations was excused playing on either Christmas Day or Good Friday. He did in fact turn out for Pompey one Christmas Day. It was the last occasion in which Pompey took part in a fixture on that date, and they lost 7-4 away to Chelsea.

JACK WARNER

Jack Warner played a vital role in Pompey's rise from the Southern League to the First Division: he was the Pompey trainer from 1919 until 1935. He joined the club from Southampton as a player in 1906, and made 227 appearances in the Southern League. He returned to Fratton Park immediately after World War I, and served under Robert Brown as Pompey won the Southern League championship in 1919/20 and became founder members of the Football League Third Division. He helped Pompey to two promotions in 1924 and 1927 under manager John McCartney, and then visited Wembley for two FA Cup Finals in 1929 and 1934 with Jack Tinn.

POMPEY CHAIRMEN

1899-1912	Sir John Brickwood
1912-1920	George Lewin Oliver
1920-1924	Rev Bruce Cornford
1924-1934	Robert Blyth
1934-1937	Alfred Hooper
1937-1940	William Kiln
1940-1945	Sydney Leverett
1945-1946	Stephen Cribb
1946-1949	Richard Vernon Stokes
1949-1951	James Chinnick
1951-1954	Richard Vernon Stokes
1954-1955	John Privett
1955-1957	Guy Spriggins
1957-1959	Jack Sparshatt
1959-1966	Dr Ian McLachlan
1966-1973	Dennis Collett
1973-1988	John Deacon
1988-1996	Jim Gregory
1996-1997	Martin Gregory
1997-1998	Terry Venables
1998	Martin Gregory
1998-1999	Les Parris
1999-2006	Milan Mandaric

LAWRENCE THE SUBSTITUTE

George Lawrence made 12 league appearances for Pompey – all as substitute. He was signed on a free transfer by Jim Smith from non-league Weymouth towards the end of the 1992/93 campaign, and made his debut in a 1-0 win away to Cambridge United on 13 March. He came off the bench in the next 11 consecutive games, and Pompey dropped only four points. He made one more appearance as a substitute in the play-off first leg – Pompey lost 1-0 to Leicester City – and made his only start in the second leg at Fratton Park, which ended 2-2.

SCORED FOR REPUBLIC OF IRELAND

The following Pompey players have scored for the Republic of Ireland:

Eoin Hand	2
Alan McLoughlin	2
Kevin O'Callaghan	1

A HAPPY BIRTHDAY

On 17 September 1947 Jack Froggatt celebrated his 25th birthday with a second-half hat trick in a 6-0 victory against Sheffield United in a First Division clash at Fratton Park. It was his first of two hat-tricks for the club.

LAST DAY ESCAPE II

5 May 1996, Division One..........................Huddersfield Town 0 Pompey 1

Pompey needed to win this game and hope Millwall would fail to beat Ipswich Town at Portman Road to avoid the drop. Huddersfield were dealt a blow after only five minutes when striker Andy Booth was carried off. Three minutes later, 19-year-old Deon Burton volleyed home the only goal of the match following a free-kick by Fitzroy Simpson. Alan Knight in the Pompey goal was not tested, and Paul Hall and Alan McLoughlin went close to increasing Pompey's lead. At Portman Road, Ipswich Town and Millwall drew 0-0, so Pompey lived to fight another season in Division One. POMPEY: Alan Knight, Jason Rees, Andy Awford, Alan McLoughlin, Andy Thomson, Guy Butters, Martin Allen, Fitzroy Simpson, Deon Burton, Paul Hall, Jimmy Carter.

WHEN DUGGIE HAD TO WATCH

Duggie Reid did not enjoy watching football, and didn't even watch his son David play – except once. He promised David, once a Pompey junior, that if ever he played at Wembley Stadium, he would be there to watch. In 1978, David reached the twin towers with Leatherhead in the FA Trophy, and Mrs Reid snr reminded Duggie he had made the promise. So Duggie went to Wembley, but unfortunately Leatherhead lost 3-1 to Altrincham. At least David, who dreamed of following his father into the Pompey team, appeared at Wembley, which was something his father never managed.

WHEN TED DRAKE LENT A HAND

Ted Drake made one wartime appearance for Pompey – and scored four goals. On Boxing Day 1945, he played at inside-right in Pompey's League South fixture at home to Crystal Palace, and his goals helped Pompey to a 9-1 victory. Three of Drake's goals came in the last seven minutes.

LEAGUE CUP APPEARANCES

Alan Knight played 53 matches for Pompey in the League Cup, and holds the club appearance record in the competition.

GOING DOWN

Pompey's 32-year spell in Division One ended in 1959. They suffered several crushing defeats, and failed to win a League match after beating Burnley 4-2 in November 1958. They went bottom of the table following a 4-4 draw against Tottenham Hotspur at White Hart Lane on 21 February, and only picked up two more points from 13 matches thereafter. Ron Saunders was top scorer with 21 League goals from 35 appearances.

Football League Division One 1958/59

	Pl	W	D	L	F	A	W	D	L	F	A	Pts
1 Wolverhampton W	42	15	3	3	68	19	13	2	6	42	30	61
2 Manchester United	42	14	4	3	58	27	10	3	8	45	39	55
3 Arsenal	42	14	3	4	53	29	7	5	9	35	39	50
4 Bolton Wanderers	42	14	3	4	56	30	6	7	8	23	36	50
5 West Bromwich Albion	42	8	7	6	41	33	10	6	5	47	35	49
6 West Ham United	42	15	3	3	59	29	6	3	12	26	41	48
7 Burnley	42	11	4	6	41	29	8	6	7	40	41	48
8 Blackpool	42	12	7	2	39	13	6	4	11	27	36	47
9 Birmingham City	42	14	1	6	54	35	6	5	10	30	33	46
10 Blackburn Rovers	42	12	3	6	48	28	5	7	9	28	42	44
11 Newcastle United	42	11	3	7	40	29	6	4	11	40	51	41
12 Preston North End	42	9	3	9	40	39	8	4	9	30	38	41
13 Nottingham Forest	42	9	4	8	37	32	8	2	11	34	42	40
14 Chelsea	42	13	2	6	52	37	5	2	14	25	61	40
15 Leeds United	42	8	7	6	28	27	7	2	12	29	47	39
16 Everton	42	11	3	7	39	38	6	1	14	32	49	38
17 Luton Town	42	11	6	4	50	26	1	7	13	18	45	37
18 Tottenham Hotspur	42	10	3	8	56	42	3	7	11	29	53	36
19 Leicester City	42	7	6	8	34	36	4	4	13	33	62	32
20 Manchester City	42	8	7	6	40	32	3	2	16	24	63	31
21 Aston Villa	42	8	5	8	31	33	3	3	15	27	54	30
22 POMPEY	42	5	4	12	38	47	1	5	15	26	65	21

A STATUETTE FOR JIMMY

Pompey and Norwich City players lined up around the centre circle to await Jimmy Dickinson when he made his last Fratton Park appearance. He was presented with a statuette by team-mate Harry Harris that read: "Presented to Jimmy Dickinson by the players and staff of Portsmouth Football Club on his retirement, in recognition of his sterling qualities as a player for Portsmouth". The Pompey team did Dickinson proud by beating Norwich 4-0.

PEDRO SPARKS REVIVAL

Pompey made certain of Premiership survival by beating Wigan Athletic 2-1 at the JJB Stadium in April 2006, but it was two goals by Pedro Mendes the previous month that sparked the revival. The club looked certain to be relegated from the Premiership at the time Manchester City visited Fratton Park on 11 March 2006. Mendes gave Pompey the lead with a spectacular effort, but their first win since New Year's Eve looked as far away as ever when Richard Dunne equalised. In the last minute, however, another super strike from the Pompey midfielder earned the much-welcome victory, and a week later he was on the score-sheet again as Pompey beat West Ham United 4-2 to record their first win at Upton Park since October 1929.

GRAY'S "HAT-TRICK"

When Pompey lost 2-1 to Crystal Palace at Selhurst Park on 8 April 1986, Andy Gray scored all three goals. He headed Crystal Palace into the lead on 18 minutes, then a hit-and-hope shot from the touchline gave his side a 2-0 advantage. In the second half, his diving header diverted Mick Kennedy's shot past his own goalkeeper.

SHORT-TERM MANAGERS

The following men, all associated with Pompey, have been managers for a matter of days. Former player Paul Went took charge of Orient and lasted only 19 days in the job, leaving in October 1981. Terry Fenwick, Pompey manager from January 1995 to January 1998, was boss of Northampton Town for 49 days before departing in February 2003. Steve Wicks, who assisted Pompey boss John Gregory in 1989, left Lincoln City after being in charge for 41 days, and Steve Claridge became manager of Millwall on 20 June 2005, only to be sacked before the new season had even begun.

FULHAM BEAT POMPEY AT LAST

Up until the 1972/73 season, Pompey and Fulham had met in the Football League on 16 occasions. Pompey had by far enjoyed the best of the exchanges, having won eleven and drawn five. The two sides drew 0-0 at Craven Cottage in their 17th meeting, but on 21 April 1973 at Fratton Park, Fulham at last got the better of Pompey, winning 2-1.

FIRST PENALTY SHOOT-OUT

The 1992 replay between Liverpool and Pompey was the first occasion that an FA Cup semi-final was decided on a penalty shoot-out.

ONE-MATCH WONDERS

Since Pompey became members of the Football League in 1920, fifty players have made just one appearance in a competitive match for the Club. In chronological order they are:

Bert Youtman	1920/21
John Smelt	1920/21
Bob Cringan	1921/22
Moses Edwards	1921/22
Harry Moore	1923/24
Arthur Foxall	1924/25
Ted Hough	1931/32
Bill O'Hare	1931/32
Willie Bell	1931/32
Bill Kennedy	1931/32
Jack Friar	1932/33
Jessie Weekes	1932/33
Rod Welch	1932/33
Len Williams	1933/34
Bill Clarke	1934/35
Bob Muir	1934/35
Ambrose Brown	1935/36
Tom Hird	1935/36
Reg Gundry	1935/36
Brian Dalton	1935/36
Harry Crawshaw	1936/37
Eric Jones	1937/38
John Crossley	1945/46
Jack Foxton	1946/47
George Hudson	1946/47
Ian Drummond	1947/48
Harry Lunn	1947/48
Jimmy Dawson	1949/50
Jimmy Elder	1949/50
Peter Higham	1949/50
Brian Edwards	1951/52
Rodney Henwood	1953/54
Charlie Mortimore	1953/54
Ivor Evans	1956/57
Jimmy Clugston	1956/57
Colin Osmond	1957/58
Dennis Davidson	1959/60
Bob Gaddes	1959/60

John Fraser 1960/61
John Ashworth 1962/63
Derek Gamblin 1965/66
Paul Smith 1973/74
Paul Bennett 1976/77
David Leworthy 1981/82
Liam Daish 1986/87
Roy Young 1993/94
Aaron Cook 1997/98
Paul Harries 1997/98
Anthony Fenton 1999/2000
Anthony Pulis 2004/05

FANATICAL DAUGHTER

Lesley Stephen, daughter of 1950s full-back Jimmy Stephen, is a Fratton Park season-ticket holder but has been more than just a Pompey fan over many years. She was once secretary of Pompey Young Supporters' Club and was also secretary of the 1976 SOS Pompey Appeal.

SAVED BY THE WHISTLE

Pompey were saved from defeat by the referee's whistle when they met Crystal Palace in a First Division fixture on 23 March 1996. The score was 0-0 when, after five minutes of added-on time, Andy Roberts's shot screamed past Alan Knight for what would have been the winning goal for Palace... but referee Alan Wiley blew for full-time before the ball had crossed the line.

SWIFT FAINTS

19-year-old Manchester City goalkeeper Frank Swift fainted after the 1934 FA Cup Final, in which his side beat Pompey 2-1. A year earlier, he had watched City lose 3-0 to Everton from behind the goal at Wembley.

ALL HOME TIES

When Pompey won the FA Cup in 1939 all the ties (except the semi-final and final) were played at Fratton Park:

Round 3 .... Lincoln City 4-0
Round 4 .... West Bromwich Albion 2-0
Round 5 .... West Ham United 2-0
Round 6 .... Preston North End 1-0

FACED POMPEY IN CUP FINAL

John McClelland's father Jim faced Pompey in the 1929 FA Cup Final. He played at inside-right for Bolton Wanderers, who beat Pompey 2-0.

QUICK MARCH

In 1949, the famous Pompey Chimes were set to music by Sir Vivian Dunn, Principal Director of Music of the Royal Marines, and this was released on a 78rpm record. Unfortunately there are very few copies of the record now in existence.

POMPEY'S BUSBY BABE

Any young player to play for Manchester United during the 1950s and 1960s was known as a Busby Babe, after the club's legendary manager Matt Busby. One of the babes, Frank Haydock, spent three years with Pompey. As United rebuilt after the Munich air disaster in February 1958, Haydock made six appearances for the Red Devils, playing alongside the likes of Bobby Charlton, Albert Quixall and Dennis Viollet before being transferred to Charlton Athletic in August 1963. In December 1965, he moved to Fratton Park and played 79 games – all at centre-half – prior to joining Southend United in February 1969.

MARINE CHAMPIONS

During World War II, Reg Flewin was the Royal Marines' heavyweight boxing champion, while Freddie Evans was the Corps' champion sprinter.

THANKS STEVE

Steve Davey's 85th-minute equaliser at Hartlepool United on Friday 24 August 1978 saved Pompey from landing bottom of the Fourth Division. Pompey had lost their first two matches in Division Four, and were trailing 1-0 with five minutes to go at the Victoria Ground when Davey headed his first goal for the club.

NEW COACH

A new coach was built in 1974 to transport the Pompey team to away games. Byng's, a Portsmouth-based coach company, approached the club with a view to hiring it, and when they agreed, the building of the vehicle commenced immediately. The cost was £20,000, and the coach possessed a television, eight-track stereo and a deep freeze.

MOST-CAPPED GOALIE

Mart Poom is Pompey's most-capped goalkeeper. He joined Pompey in August 1994 from Swiss club FC Wil, and spent two seasons at Fratton Park. During that time, he represented Estonia on 30 occasions, and yet only made seven appearances for Pompey.

JIM FIXED IT

One of the most important matches in Pompey history occurred on 14 May 1977, when Pompey entertained York City in a Third Division relegation decider at Fratton Park. It was Jimmy Dickinson's first home match in charge, and a win over doomed York City would guarantee Pompey's survival. Two young Pompey supporters, Ian Lindsay and Derek Scott, had made a huge banner displaying the words, "Jim'll Fix It" and it was held up at the Milton End throughout the game. George Hope put York City ahead after half an hour, but two goals by Clive Green and one from David Kemp guaranteed that Third Division football would be played at Fratton Park the following season.

A REMARKABLE SUPPORTER

Mr Jim Scholes was a Pompey supporter for 55 years, and attended matches well into his eighties. What was more remarkable was that for the last 35 years of his life he was totally blind, yet he hardly missed a match at Fratton Park. He didn't "watch" games with the aid of a commentator, but was completely independent. He travelled to and from the ground on his own, and his journey required a long walk before he caught a bus. Mr Scholes always maintained he could follow a game well by the noise of the crowd, and if he needed to check anything then he only had to ask.

FRATTON IS HOME TO MILLWALL

On 1 April 1978, Millwall, banned from their own ground The Den because of crowd violence, played a home game against Bristol Rovers at Fratton Park. Rovers won the Second Division clash 3-1 before a crowd of 3,322. Meanwhile, Pompey lost 1-0 away to Bradford City in Division Three.

CHANGE OF LUCK

In 1967, Pompey abandoned their famous blue and white for an all-blue strip with red and white trimmings. The change seemed to bring the team better results, with seven points gained from their first four matches, and the 1967/68 season was the most exciting for some years.

AFTER THE LORD MAYOR'S SHOW

After taking eventual 1970/71 League and FA Cup double-winners Arsenal to a replay at Highbury and losing only to a late penalty, Pompey came crashing down to earth in their next match. They were beaten in a Second Division fixture 4-1 by Carlisle United, who recorded their first ever victory at Fratton Park. It was also the Cumbrians' first win on their travels since Boxing Day 1969.

TOP GOALSCORERS

Pompey's top league goal-scorers from their first season in the Football League until the outbreak of World War II were:

1920/21	Frank Stringfellow	13
1921/22	Percy Cherrett	22
1922/23	Jerry Mackie	11
1923/24	Billy Haines	28
1924/25	Billy Haines	17
1925/26	Billy Haines	20
1926/27	Billy Haines	40
1927/28	Billy Haines and Jack Smith	11
1928/29	Fred Forward, Jack Smith, Johnny Weddle, Bobby Irvine	8
1929/30	Johnny Weddle	20
1930/31	Johnny Weddle	24
1931/32	Johnny Weddle	22
1932/33	Johnny Weddle	20
1933/34	Johnny Weddle	17
1934/35	Johnny Weddle	24
1935/36	Johnny Weddle	16
1936/37	Johnny Weddle and Jock Anderson	10
1937/38	Jimmy Beattie	21
1938/39	Jock Anderson	10

SCORED IN ALL COMPETITIONS

Billy Eames scored three goals during the 1975/76 campaign, and each one came in a different competition. He grabbed his first on his debut, after coming on as a substitute in a League Cup second round tie against Leicester City in September 1975. His second came in the FA Cup third round against Birmingham City at Fratton Park in January 1976, and a week later he scored the only goal in the Division Two encounter with Carlisle United. This earned Pompey their first home victory of the season.

NEWTON GOES BACK

One of Alan Ball's first signings after the arrival of Milan Mandaric as the club's new owner in 1999 was midfielder Adam Newton from West Ham United. The intention was for Newton to spend a year on loan at Fratton Park, but after one month the player had only made one start for Pompey, and so Harry Redknapp, then manager of the Hammers, took him back to Upton Park.

POMPEY LINK TO CUP UPSET

In February 1971, Colchester United produced one of the biggest FA Cup shocks of all time when they beat Leeds United 3-2 at Layer Road. The Fourth Division club's side that afternoon consisted of three players with Pompey links. Former Pompey centre forward Ray Crawford scored the first two goals, Brian Lewis had spent four years at Fratton Park during the 1960s and subsequently returned, while Dave Simmonds, scorer of Colchester United's third goal, was born in Portsmouth.

HOW POMPEY SIGNED HARRY FERRIER

Harry Ferrier guested for Pompey during World War II, and after the war ended, the club paid £1,000 to sign him from Barnsley. He was at the time serving with the Royal Artillery at Woolwich, and Pompey secretary Dan Clarke, complete with signing-on papers, travelled there to meet the player, only to be told he had gone to the cinema. A notice was flashed onto the screen informing Ferrier to telephone Barnsley Football Club, and the final details of the transfer were completed in a telephone kiosk.

COUPONS APPEAL

In 1945, with clothes rationing in force, the club appealed to supporters for 500 clothing coupons. Enough came in to buy a new strip to begin the 1945/46 campaign, and every supporter who made a donation received a letter of thanks from secretary-manager Jack Tinn.

MONTY'S ORDER, "SIGN REID"

Duggie Reid was one of the club's finest ever players, and they had reason to thank the club president Field Marshal Montgomery for that. Reid served in the army at El Alamein, and took part in many football matches that were witnessed by Monty. He was on the books of Stockport County, but after the war a host of top clubs were looking to acquire his signature. It was because of Montgomery's recommendation that Reid ended up signing for Pompey.

POMPEY WORLD CUP PLAYERS

The following Pompey players have represented their countries in the World Cup Finals. The amount of matches played at each tournament is shown in brackets:

Jimmy Dickinson ....England 1950 (2) 1954 (3)
Paul Hall ....Jamaica 1998 (3)
Fitzroy Simpson ....Jamaica 1998 (3)
Norman Uprichard......Northern Ireland ....(2)
Derek Dougan ....Northern Ireland ....(1)

HALF A MATCH, HALF A PITCH

Thick fog caused the Isle of Wight ferries to be suspended on 13 March 1948, but that didn't prevent Mr Gordon Holmes and his young son Colin getting to Fratton Park to watch Pompey play Blackpool. Being told at Sandown Railway Station that all ferries were cancelled, they travelled to Ryde in the hope that the fog may have cleared a little. The fog was even more dense at Ryde, but they heard a man offering trips to Portsmouth in a small boat and took up his offer, paying five times the amount of the normal fare. They reached Fratton Park at half-time, squeezing in at the back of the Fratton End, but could only see as far as the half-way line. They arrived home at midnight after seeing half a match on half a pitch.

KELLY ARGUMENT

At 18 years old, Mark Kelly had won a full international cap, and even prior to that had been the cause of an argument between the Football Associations of both England and the Republic of Ireland. He had made his international debut for the Republic of Ireland Youth team, but a month later was named in the English squad that was to face Denmark. The Football Association of Ireland claimed that he had already played for them, while the English argued that he had no Irish passport. As Kelly's father was born in Dublin, the Irish won the day, and he gained his first cap in April 1988 when the Republic of Ireland beat Yugoslavia 2-0.

BESIDE THE SEASIDE

The reason Ernie Butler was the Pompey goalkeeper throughout the club's glory years of 1948-1950 was that Portsmouth was by the sea. Attracting the attention of league clubs with his displays for Bath City, he finally had the choice of three clubs, but chose Pompey because he loved the sea air.

TRAINING GROUND

Pompey have been searching for a training ground for some years, but the irony is that they once had one. In 1958, the club acquired a derelict site in Tamworth Road, about a mile from Fratton Park, and employed former player Duggie Reid to oversee the ground's development. Eventually, dressing-rooms and a clubhouse were built, a fence was put around the perimeter of the pitch, and youth and 'A' team matches were played there. The club sold the ground in 1965 after the decision was made to scrap the club's youth policy.

TON-UP HIRON

Ray Hiron scored his 100th goal for Pompey with a classic diving header in a 2-0 home win over Nottingham Forest in Division Two on 17 February 1973. Two minutes before half-time, with Pompey leading 1-0, he dived full-length to head home Ken Foggo's cross from the right. It was almost a carbon-copy of his first goal, against Leyton Orient in a 1-1 draw, again in the Second Division, on 12 December 1964. On that occasion, John McClelland crossed from the right and Hiron flashed home an unstoppable header to give Pompey a 1-0 lead.

McLAUGHLIN'S ONLY GOAL

Pompey began their 1979/80 Fourth Division promotion campaign with a 3-0 victory away to Hartlepool United, and John McLaughlin celebrated his club debut by scoring the second goal. He spent five years with Pompey, making 197 League and Cup appearances, but never again found the net.

A HAPPY EASTER

It was certainly a happy Easter for Pompey in 1957. They entered the holiday programme in 21st place, four points behind Cardiff City with only four matches to play, but gained maximum points from their three games. A Peter Harris goal was enough to beat Cardiff at Fratton Park on Good Friday, and the next day at Fratton, Wolverhampton Wanderers were beaten 1-0 thanks to a goal by Ron Newman. On Easter Monday, Pompey travelled to Ninian Park for the return game with Cardiff, and Peter Harris scored twice in a 2-0 win. This meant that relegation would be decided on the final day of the season, and although Pompey lost 1-0 at home to West Bromwich Albion, Cardiff's 3-2 defeat at home to Manchester United meant the Welshmen were relegated to the Second Division with Charlton Athletic.

DAVE GUNTER

Dave Gunter was the brother of Phil, a Pompey defender between 1951 and 1964, and also the son-in-law of pre-war player Bill Bagley. Dave was on Pompey's books as an amateur in the 1950s, but was not taken on as a professional, so he joined Southampton, for whom he made seven appearances in Division Three (South). In 1983, he became involved with the Pompey Young Blues, but after more than 15 years' service, he was a victim of cuts during the time the club was in administration.

FIRST LEAGUE WIN AT ST. ANDREWS

It took Pompey 21 years before they beat Birmingham City at St. Andrews. They first played on the ground on 7 April 1928, and were beaten 2-0. By the time Birmingham were relegated in 1939, Pompey had taken one point off them in 12 visits. After the war, Pompey lost at St. Andrews in one First Division match and two third round FA Cup ties before they claimed their first away victory over Birmingham, winning 3-0 on 8 October 1949.

MANLEY INJURY

In December 1973, worried by the number of goals being conceded, Pompey chairman John Deacon made £200,000 available for the club to sign central defenders Paul Went from Fulham and Malcolm Manley from Leicester City. In the 15th match of their partnership, Manley suffered a serious knee injury during an away game with Notts County, and despite featuring in one more Pompey match, he was forced to retire.

THEY'VE ALL PLAYED IN GOAL

The following goalkeepers have all represented Pompey in league matches: Ned Robson, Tommy Newton, Dan McPhail, Sandy Kane, John Jarvie, Ben Lewis, Jock Gilfillan, Jock McHugh, Cyrille Jolliffe, Bob Muir, Jimmy Strong, Harry Walker, Jim Hall, Ernie Butler, Ron Humpston, Maurice Leather, Charlie Dore, Norman Uprichard, Ted Platt, Mervyn Gill, Alan Barnett, Ray Drinkwater, Fred Brown, Dick Beattie, Bob Gaddes, John Milkins, Peter Shearing, John Armstrong, Ray Potter, Jim Standen, Graham Horn, Ron Tilsed, David Best, Phil Figgins, Grahame Lloyd, Steve Middleton, Alan Knight, Peter Mellor, Andy Gosney, Brian Horne, Mart Poom, Jimmy Glass, Aaron Flahavan, Andy Petterson, Russell Hoult, Chris Tardif, Dave Beasant, Sasa Ilic, Yoshi Kawaguchi, Shaka Hislop, Harald Wapenaar, Pavel Srnicek, Kostas Chalkias, Jamie Ashdown, Sander Westerveld, Dean Kiely.

GOING DOWN II

Two years after suffering relegation from the First Division in 1959, Pompey slipped into Division Three. They failed to win in 14 league and cup matches, from Boxing Day 1960 until Leeds United were beaten 3-1 at Fratton Park on 18 March 1961. Manager Freddie Cox was sacked during the season, and caretaker-manager Bill Thompson made two inspired signings, in the shape of Allan Brown and former Fratton favourite Johnny Gordon, before George Smith took over the reins. The team collected ten points from their last nine games, but a 3-0 defeat away to Middlesbrough consigned them to relegation.

Football League Division Two 1960-61

	Pl	W	D	L	F	A	W	D	L	F	A	Pts
1 Ipswich Town	42	15	3	3	55	24	11	4	7	45	31	59
2 Sheffield United	42	16	2	3	49	22	10	4	7	32	29	58
3 Liverpool	42	14	5	2	49	21	7	5	9	38	37	52
4 Norwich City	42	15	3	3	46	20	5	6	10	24	33	49
5 Middlesbrough	42	13	6	2	44	20	5	6	10	39	54	48
6 Sunderland	42	12	5	4	47	24	5	8	8	28	36	47
7 Swansea Town	42	14	4	3	49	26	4	7	10	28	47	47
8 Southampton	42	12	4	5	57	35	6	4	11	27	46	44
9 Scunthorpe United	42	9	8	4	39	25	5	7	9	30	39	43
10 Charlton Athletic	42	12	3	6	60	42	4	8	9	37	49	43
11 Plymouth Argyle	42	13	4	4	52	32	4	4	13	29	50	42
12 Derby County	42	9	6	6	46	35	6	4	11	34	45	40
13 Luton Town	42	13	5	3	48	27	2	4	15	23	52	39
14 Leeds United	42	7	7	7	41	38	7	3	11	34	45	38
15 Rotherham United	42	9	7	5	37	24	3	6	12	28	40	37
16 Brighton & Hove A.	42	9	6	6	33	26	5	3	13	28	49	37
17 Bristol Rovers	42	13	4	4	52	35	2	3	16	21	57	37
18 Stoke City	42	9	6	6	39	26	3	6	12	12	33	36
19 Leyton Orient	42	10	5	6	31	29	4	3	14	24	49	36
20 Huddersfield Town	42	7	5	9	33	33	6	4	11	29	38	35
21 POMPEY	42	10	6	5	38	27	1	5	15	26	64	33
22 Lincoln City	42	5	4	12	30	43	3	4	14	18	52	24

CHIEF SCOUT AT 28

Andy Awford became the youngest chief scout in Pompey history when on 1 December 2000 he was appointed at the age of 28. Awford, who was only 16 when he made the first of 372 Pompey appearances, had suffered two broken legs during his career and decided to retire from the game.

ONLY REID

Duggie Reid was the only Pompey player to score a hat trick in the Football League in the first five seasons after World War II. He hit seven trebles in all, the first in the penultimate game of the 1946/47 season as Pompey beat Chelsea 4-1 at Stamford Bridge. He netted his first treble at Fratton Park in a 4-0 victory over Grimsby Town in November 1947, then scored all three goals in a home win over Charlton Athletic in September 1948. During 1949/50, he recorded three hat tricks. His first of the season came in a 7-0 thrashing of Everton at Fratton Park in September 1949, and there were three more in a 4-0 win at home to Chelsea in March 1950. His most important hat trick came on the last day of the 1949/50 campaign, for the League Championship was decided when Pompey beat Aston Villa 5-1 at home. Reid's final hat trick came in September 1950, against Stoke City who were beaten 5-1 on their visit to Fratton Park.

TOP GOALSCORERS II

Pompey's top league goalscorers from 1946/47 to 1958/59 were:

1946/47	Duggie Reid	29
1947/48	Duggie Reid	14
1948/49	Peter Harris	18
1949/50	Ike Clarke	17
1950/51	Duggie Reid	21
1951/52	Duggie Reid	16
1952/53	Peter Harris	23
1953/54	Peter Harris	20
1954/55	Johnny Gordon	13
1955/56	Peter Harris	23
1956/57	Peter Harris	13
1957/58	Peter Harris	18
1958/59	Ron Saunders	21

SCOULAR MAKES FA CUP HISTORY

In 1946, Jimmy Scoular made history by becoming the first player to play for two different clubs in the same FA Cup competition. He played in Pompey's 1-0 defeat away to Birmingham City in the third round first leg, having appeared for Gosport Borough in a preliminary round. The only other player to later play for two different clubs was Stan Crowther, who was allowed to represent Manchester United in the 1958 FA Cup Final, since United had lost so many players in the Munich air disaster. He had earlier played for Aston Villa.

JIMMY DICKINSON

The name Jimmy Dickinson is the most famous in the history of Portsmouth Football Club. Universally known as Gentleman Jim, he was never spoken to by a referee, let alone booked or sent off in a 20-year career that won him two Football League Championship medals, a Third Division Championship medal and 48 England caps. He was born in Alton, and attended the town's Senior Boys' School. He was spotted playing football in the playground there by teacher Eddie Lever, who would one day be his manager at Fratton Park. In 1943, Lever recommended to Jack Tinn that Dickinson be given a trial, and on 1 May 1943, Dickinson played in a friendly against Reading that Pompey won 4-2. The press reported that he "gave a good account of himself." When League football resumed in 1946, Pompey's first opponents were Blackburn Rovers at Fratton Park, and Dickinson played at right-half in a 3-1 win. He soon switched to left-half, and held the position for the rest of the season, missing just two games. He was ever-present throughout 1947/48, and missed only three matches over the next two seasons, both of which ended in League titles for the club. His contribution to the team's success could have been overlooked compared to the skills of other stars in the side such as Jimmy Scoular, Peter Harris, and Len Phillips, but it was Dickinson who displayed supreme consistency. He was appointed captain in 1953, but the great side was breaking up, and he found himself leading a team that each year took a step closer to Division Two. The club was relegated in 1959, and two years later slipped into the Third Division. Dickinson led the club back to Division Two at the first attempt, and played his 764th and final league match on his 40th birthday at Northampton Town. Pompey drew 1-1 to avoid being relegated back to the Third Division. He took the job as Public Relations Officer at Fratton Park, and was later appointed secretary, but in 1977 became manager of the club. After Pompey drew 1-1 at Barnsley on 30 March 1979, he suffered a major heart attack in the dressing-room and resigned two months later on health grounds. He died on 8 November 1982, aged 57. There are plans to erect a statue of Jimmy Dickinson when Fratton Park is finally redeveloped.

LARGE SET OF CLUBS

Steve Claridge began his football life as an apprentice with Pompey and has turned out for 13 different league clubs throughout a long career. They are: Bournemouth, Aldershot, Cambridge United, Luton Town, Birmingham City, Leicester City, Pompey, Wolverhampton Wanderers, Millwall, Brighton and Hove Albion, Brentford, Wycombe Wanderers and Bradford City.

SO CLOSE TO BEATING ARSENAL

Pompey went close to beating Arsenal in January 1988, when the
Gunners visited Fratton Park for a league match for the first time in 28
years. Three minutes from the end, with the score at 1-1, Pompey were
awarded a penalty, but John Lukic produced a great full-length save to
deny Kevin Dillon.

PROPERTY DEVELOPERS

On 27 November 2003, the club revealed plans to build hundreds of
homes. It was announced that the £90m scheme would pay for the £36m
ground to be built alongside it on the existing Fratton Park.

ROOKES THE ENTREPRENEUR

In 1948, Pompey right-back Phil Rookes hit on an idea to earn some extra
money for himself and his team-mates. With the club's permission, he
approached Portsmouth-based photographers Wright and Logan and
arranged for head-and-shoulder photographs of all the players, plus a
team photo, to be taken. The photographs were sold outside Fratton Park
on match-days, and the profits shared among the players.

GREAT COMEBACK

One of the most exciting Pompey comebacks took place at Fratton Park
on 10 September 1955. Trailing 3-0 to Bolton Wanderers with 13 minutes
to go, Pat Neil pulled a goal back, then Peter Harris scored twice to earn
the Blues an unlikely point.

FRIEND NOT FOE

Marc-Vivien Foe was on the brink of signing for Pompey when he
collapsed and died of a heart attack during Cameroon's match against
Columbia in Lyon on 26 June 2003.

UNITED STATES HALL OF FAME

In 1967, former Pompey player Ron Newman moved to the United States
of America to play for Atlanta Chiefs in the National Professional Soccer
League. He later took over as manager of Dallas Tornado, Fort
Lauderdale, Diego Sockers and Kansas City Wizards and achieved
success with all four clubs. In 1992, he was inducted into the United
States Soccer Hall of Fame.

THREE OFF

Pompey had three players sent off in a Second Division match against Sheffield United at Bramall Lane on 13 December 1986. Billy Gilbert saw red for dissent, Kevin Dillon was sent off for two bookings, and Mick Tait received his marching orders for an off-the-ball incident involving Blades' Peter Beagrie, who was also ordered off.

POMPEY HUMBLE THE CHAMPS

On 3 September 1955, Pompey produced one of their greatest performances of all time when they defeated reigning League Champions Chelsea 5-1 at Stamford Bridge. Peter Harris lobbed in Pompey's first goal on 20 minutes, and a superb shot by Jackie Henderson doubled the lead before Derek Rees slotted home the third in the 42nd minute. Rees made it four after the break, but with seven minutes to go, Chelsea's Seamus O'Connell pulled a goal back. Peter Harris restored Pompey's four-goal advantage, and Pat Neil went close to grabbing a sixth goal.

TOP GOALKEEPERS

The five goalkeepers who have made the most league appearances for Pompey are:

Alan Knight	683
John Milkins	344
Jock Gilfillan	330
Ernie Butler	222
Norman Uprichard	162

LEVERETT HOUSE

In 1958, Pompey opened a hostel for young players and named it Leverett House, after Sydney Leverett who had been a director of the club since 1912. The house, approximately two miles from Fratton Park, was on four floors, and housed 15 players plus wardens' accommodation. Duggie Reid and his wife Mary were wardens of the home until it was sold in 1965, when the club made the decision to abolish the youth and reserve set-up.

WIN OVER SAINTS

On 21 March 2004 a goal by Yakubu Ayegbeni was enough to secure Pompey's first home win over neighbours Southampton since 1963. The victory was the start of an eight-match unbeaten run.

DUNCAN GILCHRIST

Duncan Gilchrist died after heading a ball in a reserve match at Gosport in March 1924. The coroner's verdict was accidental death, so as Portsmouth Football Club had no legal claim on the Football League Insurance Fund, the League made an ex-gratia payment of £100 to the directors, with instructions to administer the sum as they thought fit. It was agreed at a board meeting that the money be sent to the player's mother.

THEY COULDN'T BELIEVE IT

Tottenham Hotspur supporters thought the scoreline should have been the opposite way round in January 1937 when they heard that their team had beaten Pompey 5-0 at Fratton Park in the FA Cup third round. Pompey were then seventh in the First Division, while Spurs occupied 11th place in Division Two.

WHAT A GUY

Guy Whittingham scored hat-tricks for Pompey in consecutive FA Cup ties. In the third round in January 1991, he scored three times in a 5-0 victory at non-league Barnet, and bagged four second-half goals in the fourth round as AFC Bournemouth were beaten 5-1.

PREKI DEBUT DELAYED

Pompey manager Jim Smith had high hopes of Preki when he bought him from Everton for £100,000 in July 1994. Unfortunately, his Pompey debut was delayed for a month, because 48 hours before the new season kicked off he fell over a ball on the training ground and broke his arm.

TWO APPEARANCE RECORDS

Jimmy Dickinson held two appearance records when he retired from the game in 1965. His 764 games were a Football League record, and they were also played for one club. The overall record was beaten in 1975, when Terry Paine turned out for Hereford United in their Third Division home fixture with Peterborough United. John Trollope overtook the one-club record when he played his 765th league game for Swindon Town at home to Carlisle United in October 1980. However, under different circumstances, Dickinson might still have held the one-club appearance record. In his day, international matches often clashed with Football League fixtures, and he played for England on 12 occasions when Pompey would have been glad of his services.

IF I SHOULD GO

After Pompey were thrashed 5-0 by Nottingham Forest at the City Ground in November 1987, chairman John Deacon was abused by a section of Pompey supporters, but hit back with the blunt message: "If I go, the club goes". At the time, Mr Deacon owned 193,001 of the 250,000 shares, and his loans to the club stood at £350,000.

FUNDRAISING FRIENDLY

On 17 August 1982 Pompey and Coventry City drew 1-1 in a friendly at Fratton Park. The match was staged to raise money for the South Atlantic Fund in memory of men whose lives were lost when HMS Coventry was sunk during the Falklands crisis. A crowd of 3,066 watched the match and over £5,000 was raised.

BEST 4 x 4

Four players have scored four goals against Pompey in the Football League at Fratton Park.

Harry Kirk ....03/03/1924 ..Pompey 3 Exeter 4 ..Division Three (South)
David Halliday ......18/02/1928 ..Pompey 3 Sunderland 5 ....Division One
Alec Gardiner ....21/02/1934 ..Pompey 3 Leicester City 5 ......Division One
Bobby Davidson ..12/12/1936 ..Pompey 1 Arsenal 5 ....Division One

SEE YOU NEXT WEEK

In the 1978/79 season, Pompey met both their FA Cup opponents in the league the following week. They beat Northampton Town 2-0 in the first round at Fratton Park in November, and won by the same scoreline in a Fourth Division clash at the County Ground the following Saturday. They then lost 1-0 at home to Reading in the second round, but gained revenge on the Royals' return to Fratton Park seven days later, winning 4-0.

WIN OVER THE BABES

Pompey's last match against the Busby Babes before the Munich air disaster of February 1958 ended in a 3-0 win at Old Trafford. On 19 October 1957, Jackie Henderson gave Pompey an early lead, then two goals in the last three minutes of the first-half by Ron Newman and Peter Harris secured a great victory over the reigning League Champions. Four of the Manchester United side that day, Mark Jones, Eddie Colman, Billy Whelan, and David Pegg, perished at Munich.

POP GROUP

Two Pompey juniors were part of a Portsmouth pop group at the beginning of the 1960s. Bobby Ridley was a singer, and Bill Williams played the guitar. The group performed regularly at hospitals and youth clubs in the Portsmouth area.

LONG WAIT FOR LIVE MATCH

Pompey were shown live on television for the first time when they faced Liverpool in the FA Cup semi-final at Highbury on 5 April 1992.

TINDALL'S VISION

In 1966, Ron Tindall devised a new points plan, and submitted the system to the Football League. The idea was that the team that led at half-time would receive two points, as would the winners of the second period. One point each would be given to sides that drew the first half, second half or overall. He received no reply from the Football League, but the system was used in a Western Australia Summer Night Series in 1978.

KENNEDY FINED

In August 1987, Pompey midfielder Mick Kennedy was fined £5,000 – the heaviest fine in the history of English football to that date. He appeared at Lancaster Gate on a charge of bringing the game into disrepute, following two controversial articles that appeared in *The Sun* newspaper. In the articles, Kennedy claimed that he was the hardest man in soccer and enjoyed hurting opponents. He also boasted he "took no prisoners", and accused top players of being chicken.

EUROPEAN CHAMPION

Tony Barton is the only former Pompey player to manage a European Cup-winning side. He achieved the feat in 1982, when his Aston Villa side beat Bayern Munich 1-0 in Rotterdam.

FOUR ON HOME DEBUT

On 20 March 1925, Harry Havelock scored four goals on his home debut for Pompey. He had made two appearances in away games before Pompey faced Nottingham Forest in the Second Division at Fratton Park, and he scored a first-half hat trick, later adding another goal as Pompey won 5-1.

WE ARE THE CHAMPIONS III

Pompey won the Third Division championship in 1961/62 at the first attempt. They remained unbeaten until losing 2-1 away to Notts County in their 13th match, and their experienced side won the league by five points, making sure of the title by beating Watford 2-1 at home on Easter Monday. Skipper Jimmy Dickinson was the only ever-present in the side, and Ron Saunders, who scored 26 League goals, topped the goalscoring charts for the fourth successive season.

Football League Division Three 1961/62

	Pl	W	D	L	F	A	W	D	L	F	A	Pts
1 POMPEY	46	15	6	2	48	23	12	5	6	39	24	65
2 Grimsby Town	46	18	3	2	49	18	10	3	10	31	38	62
3 Bournemouth	46	14	8	1	42	18	7	9	7	27	27	59
4 Queens Park Rangers	46	15	3	5	65	31	9	8	6	46	42	59
5 Peterborough	46	16	0	7	60	38	10	6	7	47	44	58
6 Bristol City	46	15	3	5	56	27	8	5	10	38	45	54
7 Reading	46	14	5	4	46	24	8	4	11	31	42	53
8 Northampton Town	46	12	6	5	52	24	8	5	10	33	33	51
9 Swindon Town	46	11	8	4	48	26	6	7	10	30	45	49
10 Hull City	46	15	2	6	43	20	5	6	12	24	34	48
11 Bradford Park Avenue	46	13	5	5	47	27	7	2	14	33	51	47
12 Port Vale	46	12	4	7	41	23	5	7	11	24	35	45
13 Notts County	46	14	5	4	44	23	3	4	16	23	51	43
14 Coventry City	46	11	6	6	38	26	5	5	13	26	45	43
15 Crystal Palace	46	8	8	7	50	41	6	6	11	33	39	42
16 Southend United	46	10	7	6	31	26	3	9	11	26	43	42
17 Watford	46	10	9	4	37	26	4	4	15	26	48	41
18 Halifax Town	46	9	5	9	34	35	6	5	12	28	49	40
19 Shrewsbury Town	46	8	7	8	46	37	5	5	13	27	47	38
20 Barnsley	46	9	6	8	45	41	4	6	13	26	54	38
21 Torquay United	46	9	4	10	48	44	6	2	15	28	56	36
22 Lincoln City	46	4	10	9	31	43	5	7	11	26	44	35
23 Brentford	46	11	3	9	34	29	2	5	16	19	64	34
24 Newport County	46	6	5	12	29	38	1	3	19	17	64	22

THE POMPEY SWAP SHOP

In September 1966, manager George Smith wrote to clubs asking if they would be interested in doing business with Pompey in the form of player-exchange deals. With the club still owing money to two clubs for players bought months previously, there was no cash to bring in new faces.

ROUND WITH THE HAT

In November 1975, more than a thousand people attended a public meeting at Portsmouth Guildhall, as chairman John Deacon spelled out the financial plight of the club. A collection of over £1,000 was raised.

EARLY TWO-GOAL LEAD

The earliest Pompey have taken a two-goal lead is four minutes. This occurred on 27 October 1962, when Tony Barton shot them ahead in the second minute of their Second Division home clash with Bury. David Dodson followed up with a goal two minutes later. That was the end of Pompey's scoring for the day – they won the match 2-1.

DEATH OF BOB KEARNEY

In February 1931, Portsmouth Football Club were shocked by the death of centre-half Bob Kearney. Pompey were due to play West Bromwich Albion at Fratton Park in the FA Cup fifth round, and Kearney had not missed a match all season, but was one of several players doubtful for the match because of an outbreak of influenza at the club. All the players declared themselves fit to play, but were beaten 1-0 by their Second Division opponents. Far more seriously, Kearney was taken seriously ill after the game, and died a week later aged 27. The club instantly set up an appeal fund for the player's widow and child, and when it closed in April 1931, it had raised almost £1700.

MOATS AT FRATTON PARK

In 1974, Pompey were the first club to build moats behind both goals following the recommendation of Sports Minister Dennis Howell. This followed a series of pitch invasions throughout the country.

EARLY SENDING-OFF

The second Football League match to be played at Fratton Park produced a sending-off. Harry Higginbotham of Luton Town was ordered off after fouling Pompey's Joe Turner in a Division Three (South) fixture in September 1920, which Pompey won 3-0.

NORTH STAND SEATS

During the 1951 close season, 4,226 seats were installed in the North Stand. Three-quarters of these were available as season-tickets.

A NEW STADIUM

Plans for a new stadium for Pompey have been discussed since the 1940s, but the first real hint of moving to a new site surfaced in the early 1970s, when it looked possible that the club might move to the old airport. In 1989, chairman Jim Gregory earmarked the Fratton Goods Yard as a site for a £10m community stadium, but the site owners – British Rail Property Board and the National Freight Corporation – blocked the plan. Then in 1992, a year after Lord Justice Taylor's report requiring top clubs to be all-seater by 1994, Mr Gregory planned to develop Fratton Park, but he abandoned those plans after a government inspector threw out an appeal to build a new stand at the Milton End. In 1993, the club confirmed that Farlington playing fields was the chosen site for a £20m 22,500 all-seater stadium, plus 140,000 square feet of retail alongside, but again a government inspector rejected the idea. Since then, plans have been drawn up for a new ground adjacent to the existing Fratton Park, and the most recent scheme is to turn the pitch 90 degrees and build a 28,000-capacity stadium.

BRICKIE BURNS

In April 1991 Chris Burns quit his life as a bricklayer to sign for Pompey. The club paid a £25,000 fee to Vauxhall Conference side Cheltenham Town for the midfield player, and he was selected for the following season's opening game away to Blackburn Rovers. He played in all but four of the side's 46 league fixtures in 1991/92, as well as appearing in the two epic FA Cup semi-finals against Liverpool.

ONLY TWO KEEPERS

No goalkeeper other than Alan Knight and Andy Gosney played in goal for Pompey between August 1981 and August 1993. Knight was chosen as first-choice custodian at the start of the 1981/82 campaign, and Gosney was his deputy for all of those 12 years. Gosney was transferred to Birmingham City in the summer of 1993, and his place was taken by Brian Horne, who made his Pompey debut in a 1-1 draw away to Grimsby Town in August of that year.

DOUBLES

No team did the double over Pompey during the First Division title-winning season of 2002/03, but they achieved it against nine clubs. They were Bradford City, Burnley, Derby County, Gillingham, Grimsby Town, Millwall, Nottingham Forest, Rotherham United and Walsall.

DOUBLE TOPS

David Kemp didn't spend an entire season with Pompey, yet was top goal-scorer for them in two consecutive campaigns. He signed from Crystal Palace in November 1976, and topped the scoring charts with 17 that season. When he left for Carlisle United in March 1978, he was leading scorer with 21 goals, and by the time the season ended no player came near that figure.

WORLD CUP GOALKEEPERS

Two former Pompey goalkeepers took part in the 2006 World Cup finals in Germany, Yoshikatsu Kawaguchi for Japan and Shaka Hislop for Trinidad and Tobago. Hislop, at 37, was the oldest player in the tournament.

FIRST FOUR-FIGURE RECEIPTS

The FA Cup first round tie between Pompey and Manchester United on 12 January 1912 attracted a crowd of 24,329 to Fratton Park, and gate receipts – £1,101/10/0 – reached four figures for the first time. The match ended in a 2-2 draw, and Pompey won the replay 2-1.

NOT THEM AGAIN

Pompey were drawn against Swindon Town in the League Cup three seasons running – and lost them all. In 1977, the two sides drew 1-1 at Fratton Park in the third round, with Swindon winning the replay at the County Ground 4-3. The two sides met at Fratton Park for the first round first leg in August 1978, drawing 0-0 – Swindon won the second leg 4-2. The Robins made it three out of three in 1979 with a 2-0 victory at the County Ground, after Fratton Park staged a 1-1 draw in the first leg.

MANAGERS IN THE CUP FINAL

The following Pompey managers have appeared in the FA Cup Final:

Shaka Hislop	West Ham	2006
Ian St John	Liverpool	1965
Alan Ball	Everton	1968
	Arsenal	1972
Graham Rix	Arsenal	1979
	Arsenal	1980
Terry Fenwick	Queens Park Rangers	1982
John Gregory	Queens Park Rangers	1982

DURABLE BILL

Right-back Bill Probert was the only player to appear in all the club's matches of the Southern League championship-winning season (1919/20) and the first Football League campaign (1920/21).

EX-POMPEY PROFESSIONAL REUNION CLUB

The Pompey Ex-Professional Reunion Club began in 1963, after Peter Harris brought together a team of former Pompey players to play in a charity match. It was the first of many such games – on 16 September 1963, the Ex-Pompey Championship and Professional XI was registered as a bona fide football club. It was intended that the club would play for five years, but instead it continued for 30, eventually ceasing in 1993. During these three decades, many thousands of pounds were raised for charities, and even Portsmouth Football Club benefited during the financially-stricken years of the mid-1970s. Although the club no longer plays for charity, it continues to hold an annual dinner for former players and their wives, under the new name of the Pompey Ex-Professionals Reunion Club.

HILLIER OFF ON DEBUT

David Hillier was sent off on his Pompey debut at Oldham Athletic on 9 November 1996. A week after his £250,000 transfer from Arsenal, the midfield player saw red in the 64th minute of a goalless draw after he stamped on Oldham's Nick Henry.

CAR ACCIDENT LEADS TO SIGNING A LEGEND

Mr Fred Prescott was on holiday in the west of England in 1923 when he met with a car accident. Delayed by this, he went to watch Frome Town in a Somerset League match, and saw Billy Haines score six goals in the home side's 8-0 win. He immediately alerted Pompey manager John McCartney, who, after watching him play only once, offered Haines professional forms. Haines went on to score 119 goals for the club, and was top scorer for five consecutive seasons during the 1920s.

WANNA LIFT?

The Pompey players arrived for the First Division clash with Wolverhampton Wanderers at Molineux in November 2002 with only 40 minutes to go before kick-off. Their coach broke down five minutes after leaving the their midlands hotel, but fortunately Paul Merson and two directors were able to ferry the players. The match result was a 1-1 draw.

GOING CONTINENTAL

In 1973, the club decided to break from tradition and drop their royal blue colours in favour of a continental-style strip. A competition was held to design the new strip, and the winner was Mr Bob Ingram, who came up with a white shirt with two vertical stripes, blue shorts, and white socks with blue and red tops. Many supporters were unhappy with the idea, and wanted to see a return to the old blue and white. When the club was relegated to the Third Division, some even blamed the new strip. The favoured blue shirts and white shorts were re-introduced for the 1976/77 campaign, but to prove the continental-style strip was not to blame for the club's ill fortune, Pompey were relegated to the Fourth Division the following season.

SCOTTISH POMPEY

To the end of the 2005/06 season, the following Pompey players have represented Scotland while with the club:

Jimmy Scoular	9
Nigel Quashie	6
Jackie Henderson	5
Richard Hughes	4
Jimmy Easson	3
Alex Wilson	1

FIRST SUNDAY MATCH

Pompey's first Sunday match was at home to Orient in the FA Cup fourth round on 27 January 1974. A bumper crowd of 32,838 watched a 0-0 draw.

ALBERT McCANN

Albert McCann gave sterling service to Pompey from 1962 until 1974. After spells with Coventry City and Luton Town, he came to Hampshire in August 1962, and played at inside-forward for the first five years at Fratton Park. Always hard working, he possessed a fine shot and scored 98 goals for Pompey, including a hat-trick in a 3-3 draw at Bristol City in October 1966. Throughout the 1967/68 campaign, he was employed in a wider role, but still managed to fire in 16 goals, his best ever tally, making him the side's leading scorer for the third successive season. In his later years with the club, he was used more in midfield, and was extremely capable of blotting out a dangerous opponent when handed a marking job. He left Fratton Park in 1974, but is still a regular sight at Pompey's home matches.

STOLEN GLOVES

During Pompey's 1-1 draw against Huddersfield Town at Leeds Road on 9 October 1982, Pompey goalkeeper Alan Knight had gloves worth £100 stolen from his goal.

BRIEF STAY

Lee Chapman was a Pompey player for five weeks. Jim Smith won the race with West Ham to sign Chapman from Leeds United in August 1993, and the striker scored twice in the season's opener – a 3-2 defeat at Oxford United. He was sent off in his first home match, and was clearly not happy at Fratton Park, so Smith alerted his West Ham counterpart Billy Bonds. By mid-September, Chapman had joined the Hammers for £250,000 – the sum Pompey had paid Leeds United.

FIRST GOAL FOR TEN YEARS

Justin Edinburgh was feeling ill before Pompey's First Division match at home to Sheffield United in 2001 but decided to play. In the 40th minute, he scored the only goal of the game – his first for ten years.

DICKINSON STAYS

Looking for a centre-forward in the autumn of 1947, Pompey manager Bob Jackson was ready to smash Pompey's transfer record by spending £17,000 on Chelsea's Tommy Lawton. Chelsea would only allow Lawton to join Pompey if Jackson was prepared to let Jimmy Dickinson move to Stamford Bridge, so the interest in Lawton was immediately dropped.

EARLY FRIENDLY

The earliest Pompey have played a pre-season friendly was in 2002, when they hosted Celtic at Fratton Park on 10 July. A crowd of 11,553 saw Celtic win 3-2, with Richard Hughes and Linvoy Primus scoring for the Blues.

PRICELESS FIRST GOAL FOR BENJANI

In January 2006, Harry Redknapp paid £4.5m for striker Benjani Mwaruwari from Auxerre. He failed to score in 14 matches, but broke his duck in his 15th appearance, away to Wigan Athletic. The goal cancelled out Henri Camara's earlier strike, and when Benjani's goalbound header was handled by Gary Teale, Matt Taylor converted the penalty to earn Pompey the win that made them safe from relegation.

FIRST SUBSTITUTE GOALKEEPER

Aaron Flahavan was Pompey's first substitute goalkeeper. Alan Knight was sent off for carrying the ball outside his penalty area in the FA Cup fourth round tie at home to Leicester City in January 1995, and Flahavan took to the field for his first taste of first-team action.

ALAN KNIGHT

Alan Knight holds the Pompey goalkeeper appearance record, and his 683 league appearances make him second only to Jimmy Dickinson. Alan grew up in Balham, south London, and as a youngster trained with Queens Park Rangers. A week's trial at Fratton Park was organised, and when it was over he was offered schoolboy forms, which he signed on his 14th birthday. At 15, he began to play for Pompey Youth in the South East Counties League, and his displays attracted the scouts of big clubs, but Knight promised he would sign apprentice forms on his 16th birthday, and duly did so. Knight made his first-team bow at Rotherham United on the final day of the 1977/78 season, and Pompey, already relegated to Division Four, won 1-0. Coincidentally, it was manager Jimmy Dickinson who handed young Knight his debut. He spent three seasons as understudy to Peter Mellor, and eventually was made first-choice keeper at the start of 1981/82. He spent the next 15 years as the regular Pompey goalkeeper and displayed remarkable consistency. He won a Third Division Championship medal in 1982/83, and was part of the side that clinched promotion to Division One in 1986/87. When Pompey began their first season back in the top flight, away to Oxford United on 15 August 1987, Knight made history by being the first Pompey player to appear in all four divisions. In January 1997, he made his 601st League appearance for the club against Grimsby Town, thus breaking Peter Bonetti's record of 600 games for Chelsea. Pompey's first match of the new millennium – a 2-0 defeat away to Norwich City – was Knight's 683rd and last, and he remained at Fratton Park in a coaching capacity until 2005.

DOUGAN THE POLITICIAN

Derek Dougan stood as an Independent in Belfast in the 1997 General Election, and in June 2006, appeared on BBC Television's *Question Time* as a member of the United Kingdom Independent Party.

FATHER AND DAUGHTER

Terry Brady has had two spells as a director of Portsmouth Football Club. His daughter Karren is Managing Director of Birmingham City.

IF POMPEY WAS YOUR GIRLFRIEND

Over the 1996/97 Christmas period, the Pompey Independent Supporters' Club produced their first magazine. In it, they claimed: "If Pompey was your girlfriend, she would have got the elbow long ago for not delivering the goods."

SON'S SHORT STAY

Len Phillips' son Lennie was appointed Pompey Youth coach in March 1983, but was replaced during the close season.

FIRST MATCH IN DIVISION ONE

On 27 August 1927, Sunderland hit back from three goals down in front of 35,106 at Roker Park to deny Pompey a victory in their first match in Division One. Freddie Cook gave Pompey a dream start, flashing a shot high into the net on four minutes, and Jerry Mackie pounced to double the advantage. Billy Haines shot through a crowd of players on 24 minutes, but Bobby Marshall pulled a goal back for the home side before half-time. After the break, Dave Halliday scored with a cross-shot, and with Sunderland going all out for the equaliser, Billy Moffat planted the ball into his own net when attempting to clear. The Pompey team was: Dan McPhail, George Clifford, Jock McColgan, Reg Davies, Harry Foxall, Billy Moffat, Fred Forward, Jerry Mackie, Billy Haines, Dave Watson, Freddie Cook.

HIGHEST NUMBER OF GOALKEEPERS

The highest number of goalkeepers to appear for Pompey during one season is four. In 1953/54 Norman Uprichard, Ted Platt, Charlie Dore and Mervyn Gill all donned the keeper's jersey, while in 2001/02 Dave Beasant, Sasa Ilic, Yoshikatsu Kawaguchi, and Chris Tardif all kept goal for the Blues.

FLEWIN SKIPPERED THE CHAMPIONS

Reg Flewin took over as skipper from Guy Wharton early in the 1946/47 campaign, and captained Pompey to their two successive League Championships in 1948/49 and 1949/50. He only missed three games in 1948/49, but was not so lucky the following year. An appendix operation caused him to miss a run of ten matches, and an eye injury meant him sitting out six end-of-season games, but he was able to return to lead the side to a 5-1 victory at home to Aston Villa and so clinch the title for a second time.

LATE END TO SEASON

The 1946/47 campaign suffered numerous postponements owing to atrocious weather conditions, and because of this, the season ended much later than usual. Pompey's final game ended in a 2-1 defeat to Derby County at Fratton Park on 31 May. This was the latest Pompey have ever played a Football League fixture.

GOING DOWN III

In 1976, Pompey were relegated to the Third Division after spending 14 consecutive seasons in Division Two. In a disappointing campaign the team only managed four home wins all season, the first not coming until January. A great escape looked possible when they won four matches out of six between mid-February and mid-March, but their fate was sealed on 6 April when a last-minute goal by Mick Channon earned Southampton a 1-0 win at Fratton Park. Leading goal-scorer for the campaign was Norman Piper with 11.

League Division Two 1975/76

	Pl	W	D	L	F	A	W	D	L	F	A	Pts
1 Sunderland	42	19	2	0	48	10	5	6	10	19	26	56
2 Bristol City	42	11	7	3	34	14	8	8	5	25	21	53
3 West Bromwich Albion	42	10	9	2	29	12	10	4	7	21	21	53
4 Bolton Wanderers	42	12	5	4	36	14	8	7	6	28	24	52
5 Notts County	42	11	6	4	33	13	8	5	8	27	28	49
6 Southampton	42	18	2	1	49	16	3	5	13	17	34	49
7 Luton Town	42	13	6	2	38	15	6	4	11	23	36	48
8 Nottingham Forest	42	13	1	7	34	18	4	11	6	21	22	46
9 Charlton Athletic	42	11	5	5	40	34	4	7	10	21	38	42
10 Blackpool	42	9	9	3	26	22	5	5	11	14	27	42
11 Chelsea	42	7	9	5	25	20	5	7	9	28	34	40
12 Fulham	42	9	8	4	27	14	4	6	11	18	33	40
13 Orient	42	10	6	5	21	12	3	8	10	16	27	40
14 Hull City	42	9	5	7	29	23	5	6	10	16	26	39
15 Blackburn Rovers	42	8	6	7	27	22	4	8	9	18	28	38
16 Plymouth Argyle	42	13	4	4	36	20	0	8	13	12	34	38
17 Oldham Athletic	42	11	8	2	37	24	2	4	15	20	44	38
18 Bristol Rovers	42	7	9	5	20	15	4	7	10	18	35	38
19 Carlisle United	42	9	8	4	29	22	3	5	13	16	37	37
20 Oxford United	42	7	7	7	23	25	4	4	13	16	34	33
21 York City	42	8	3	10	28	34	2	5	14	11	37	28
22 POMPEY	42	4	6	11	15	23	5	1	15	17	38	25

WHERE'S PLYMOUTH?

When Pompey travelled to Plymouth Argyle for a midweek Third
Division (South) fixture on 13th April 1921, they should have had plenty
of time to reach their destination considering they left Portsmouth at
8am the day before the match. However, the club's coach driver lost his
way, and the team didn't arrive at their hotel in Plymouth until midnight.
Perhaps the long journey and late night contributed to Pompey's 2-0
defeat the following day.

ODE TO JOHNNY GORDON

Pat Neil, former Pompey player and chairman of the Pompey Ex-
Professional Reunion club, wrote this poem following the death of Johnny
Gordon in May 2001:

The name of Johnny Gordon is tinged with Pompey blue,
A local lad, whose only love was football through and through.
At first he was a groundstaff boy who had a premonition,
To play for Pompey as a pro – a reasonable ambition.
He had his wish 'ere very long, soon made a good impression,
Was in the team in '51, the inside-right position.
Meanwhile his call-up papers came – by jove, it wasn't easy
Playing football and soldiers too, at R.A.O.C. Hilsea!
He soon became a regular in Pompey's first eleven,
With Phillips, Reid and Dickinson and Harris, number seven.
His dashing skills, his terrier-like play, his great determination
Won plaudits from the Pompey fans and team-mates' admiration.
On top of this, our John possessed a silky voice, and true,
A pint of beer was all he'd need to sing the whole night through.
The record books will tell no lies; John's feats are next to none.
Six hundred games, one-sixty goals, when all is said and done.
As time goes by, as good pros know, we join the older folks.
Relive those halcyon football days, the ups, the downs, the jokes.
We thank him for the good times shared, the memories of lads together,
To watch him play was quite a joy, to know him was a pleasure.
They'll miss him in the Patron's Club when matchdays come around
At Fratton Park the emerald pitch, the buzz, the crowd, the sounds.
And he was there, last match to see, the final whistle blew,
Dramatic scenes for Pompey fans, and Johnny's swansong too.
Three score years plus ten they say is our allotted time.
John shocked us all by leaving us, aged just sixty-nine
Our John could never keep to time, in this he was a dunce,
But John Duncan Sinclair Gordon, you were early – just this once!

THE FIRST FA CUP SUBSTITUTE

Alex Wilson was Pompey's first substitute in the FA Cup competition. In the third round tie against Hull City at Boothferry Park on 28 January 1967, he replaced Albert McCann, and was called upon again in the replay at Fratton Park, when Bobby Kellard was carried off after only 15 minutes.

NOT EVEN AROUND

Alan Knight's last match for Pompey was a 2-0 defeat at Norwich City on 3 January 2000. In the side that day was Jason Crowe, who hadn't been born when Knight made his league debut at Rotherham United on 29 April 1978.

TOP GOALSCORERS III

Pompey's top league goalscorers between 1959/60 and 1975/76 were:

1959/60	Ron Saunders	17
1960/61	Ron Saunders	20
1961/62	Ron Saunders	27
1962/63	Ron Saunders	19
1963/64	Ron Saunders	33
1964/65	Cliff Portwood	11
1965/66	Albert McCann	12
1966/67	Albert McCann and Ray Hiron	11
1967/68	Albert McCann	14
1968/69	Ray Hiron	17
1969/70	Ray Hiron	18
1970/71	Ray Hiron	13
1971/72	Richard Reynolds	10
1972/73	Ray Hiron and Norman Piper	8
1973/74	Ron Davies	13
1974/75	Mick Mellows	8
1975/76	Norman Piper	11

THREE AT THE WRONG END

Noel Blake scored three own goals during the 1984/85 season. The goals assisted Wimbledon, Blackburn Rovers and Brighton and Hove Albion.

TWO OFF IN SEASON OPENER

Pompey's 1996/97 season got off to a bad start. Beaten 3-1 at Bradford City, they also had Andy Awford and Aaron Flahavan sent off.

OFF TWICE

Nigel Pepper was sent off in two consecutive First Division matches between Pompey and Bradford City at Fratton Park. The Bantams' midfield player was ordered off in Pompey's 3-1 victory in March 1997, and in October of that year, he was red-carded again in a 1-1 draw.

LOW JINKS AT FRATTON

Before the England Youth international between England and Czechoslovakia at Fratton Park in November 1989, the referee noticed the crossbars were too low. Alterations were made prior to the match, which England won 1-0.

ALAIN PERRIN

Frenchman Alain Perrin was Pompey's first foreign manager. He began his coaching career with AS Nancy in 1983, as junior to Arsène Wenger. His first management appointment was with non-league Troyes AC, and he led the club to three promotions in six years and qualification for the UEFA Cup. He was sacked by the French club in January 2004, and then had a short spell with Al-Ain in the United Arab Emirates before taking over at Fratton Park in April 2005 from Velimir Zajec, who had been in temporary charge since the resignation of Harry Redknapp. Perrin's first match at the helm brought a 4-2 victory over Charlton Athletic at Fratton Park, and two weeks later Pompey thrashed Southampton at home 4-1. But only three months into the new season, Perrin was sacked. He had been in charge for just 20 League matches, and his record was four wins, six draws and ten defeats.

PETER HARRIS AUCTION

More than £14,000 was raised at an auction in Nottingham in November 2002, when a host of items belonging to Peter Harris went on sale. The pair of boots Harris wore when he scored all five goals against Aston Villa in September 1958 went for £700, and a photograph of the 1948/49 League Championship winning team, signed by Field Marshal Montgomery of Alamein, was sold for £3,100.

POMPEY COLOURS

Pompey's first colours were salmon-pink shirts and white shorts, but they changed to white shirts and dark blue shorts in 1909. It was not until 1912 that they introduced the famous blue shirts and white shorts.

SPECIAL FRIENDLIES

The 1973/74 campaign was Pompey's 75th anniversary, and to mark the occasion, friendlies were played against Arsenal and Manchester United. A disappointing crowd of 8,850 saw Pompey beat Arsenal 2-1, but 17,228 watched a 1-1 draw when Manchester United were the visitors.

BERESFORD INJURED ON DEBUT

John Beresford made his debut in a 2-2 draw at home to Watford on 27 March 1989, following a £300,000 move from Barnsley. He broke an ankle in the game and didn't feature any more that season.

SIX OF THE BEST

Pompey have scored six or more goals in a match on 14 occasions since World War II:

25/09/1947	Division One	Pompey 6 Sheffield United 0
14/04/1947	Division One	Pompey 6 Middlesbrough 1
08/01/1949	FA Cup third round	Pompey 7 Stockport County 0
10/09/1949	Division One	Pompey 7 Everton 0
03/02/1951	Division One	Pompey 6 Everton 3
09/10/1954	Division One	Pompey 6 Sheffield United 2
04/12/1954	Division One	Pompey 6 West Bromwich Albion 1
19/12/1959	Division Two	Pompey 6 Middlesbrough 3
23/10/1971	Division Two	Pompey 6 Fulham 3
25/08/1979	Division Four	Pompey 6 Scunthorpe United 1
29/12/1979	Division Four	Pompey 6 Northampton Town 1
14/03/1992	Division Two	Pompey 6 Millwall 1
08/02/2003	Division One	Pompey 6 Derby County 2
08/11/2003	Premiership	Pompey 6 Leeds United 1

WENT IS ORIENT'S YOUNGEST

Paul Went, Pompey's record signing at £154,000 in December 1973, was the youngest player to play for Orient when he made his debut against Preston North End on 4 September 1965. He was aged 15 years 327 days.

AWAY VICTORIES

Pompey gained 11 away victories as they stormed to the First Division title in 2002/03. They had only won ten matches on their travels over the previous four seasons.

QUIET PURSUITS

Jimmy Scoular, Alex Mackie, and Bobby Kellard were three of the toughest competitors to wear the Pompey shirt, and yet off the field they involved themselves in gentle pastimes. Scoular was a keen bowls player, Mackie enjoyed fishing, and Kellard liked nothing better than to paint in watercolours.

THE POMPEY CHIMES

The Pompey Chimes is football's oldest anthem, and could never be forgotten by anyone who has heard a massed Fratton choir in full voice. "Play up Pompey – Pompey Play Up" is derived from the hour chime of the Portsmouth Guildhall clock. "Play up" was a catchphrase in the early 1900s, and it was at this time the Chimes were first heard at Fratton Park.

100% FA CUP RECORD

Pompey have met four non-league teams in the FA Cup, and have won on each occasion.

15/01/1972 ....third round ....Boston United 0 Pompey 1
11/12/1976 ....second round ....Pompey 2 Minehead 1
26/11/1977 ....second round...............Pompey 3 Bideford Town 1
05/01/1991 ....second round...........................Barnet 0 Pompey 5

GEORGE SMITH

George Smith managed Pompey from 1961 to 1970. He played for Brentford and Queens Park Rangers, and his coaching career began with Ipswich Town, before becoming manager of Eastbourne United. From 1952-54 he was the first professional manager of the England youth team. In 1956 he joined Sheffield United as coach, before taking charge of Sutton United, and then Crystal Palace. When he became manager of Pompey in 1961, the team were already heading for the Third Division, but the following season he took them straight back up as champions. He turned Pompey into pioneers by introducing a one-team scheme in the cause of economy, scrapping the reserve and youth policy and working with a basic squad of players. He was unable to take the club into the First Division – the highest position the team reached under his command was fifth in Division Two in 1967/68. He took the title General Manager in 1967, but stayed in charge of the team until 1970 – when Ron Tindall arrived. Smith, whose reign was often turbulent, made a rather muted departure in April 1971. He retired to Bodmin, Cornwall, where he died aged 68 in November 1983.

HISTORY REPEATS

In 1927, Pompey pipped Manchester City by a 200th part of a goal to clinch promotion to the First Division. History almost repeated itself in 1985, when the last day of the campaign would decide which of the two clubs accompanied Oxford United and Birmingham City into the top flight. If Manchester City lost at home to Charlton Athletic, a draw would be enough to guarantee Pompey promotion. Backed by an enormous contingent of supporters, Pompey won 2-0, thanks to goals by Kevin O'Callaghan and Vince Hilaire, but Manchester City won 5-1 to repay Pompey for the events of 1927.

THE 1967/68 SEASON

Since Pompey were relegated from the First Division in 1959, they had not threatened a return until the 1967/68 campaign. They started well, going unbeaten until their tenth match, when they lost 4-1 away to Charlton Athletic. They went top of the table on 4 November, following a 3-0 home victory over Hull City, and moved three points clear of second-placed Blackpool when they defeated the Seasiders 3-1 at Fratton Park before a crowd of 35,038 on 2 December. The FA Cup also brought in big crowds to Fratton Park, with 44,050 attending the 1-0 win over Fulham in a fourth round replay, and 42,642 turning up for the fifth round tie against West Bromwich Albion, who beat Pompey 2-1. A week earlier, Pompey had lost their unbeaten home record, going down 2-1 to Birmingham City, and also lost Ray Pointer, who broke a leg. This seemed to knock the stuffing out of the side, and promotion slipped away, with the team eventually finishing in fifth position.

MANNION'S HAT-TRICKS

Middlesbrough and England inside-forward Wilf Mannion scored hat tricks against Pompey at Ayresome Park before and after World War II. On 29 March 1939, his treble helped his side to an 8-2 victory, and on 23 November 1946 he grabbed another in a 3-3 draw. Mannion had a further reason to remember Pompey with fondness: he made his debut against them as a 17-year-old in a 0-0 draw at Ayresome Park on 26 January 1938.

VERSATILE FROGGATT

There are hardly two more contrasting positions than outside-left and centre-half, yet Jack Froggatt played for England in both. He won the first two of his 13 caps in the outside-left position, then appeared nine times at centre-half before returning to the wing.

GOING DOWN IV

Five years after John Deacon took control of Portsmouth Football Club with the promise of great things, the club were relegated to the Fourth Division. During the 1977/78 season, Pompey suffered humiliating home defeats against Tranmere Rovers and Plymouth Argyle, and relegation was confirmed when they lost 2-0 at home to Oxford United on 4 April.

Football League Division Three 1977/78

	Pl	W	D	L	F	A	W	D	L	F	A	Pts
1 Wrexham	46	14	8	1	48	19	9	7	7	30	26	61
2 Cambridge United	46	19	3	1	49	11	4	9	10	23	40	58
3 Preston North End	46	16	5	2	48	19	4	11	8	15	19	56
4 Peterborough United	46	15	7	1	32	11	5	9	9	15	22	56
5 Chester City	46	14	8	1	41	24	2	14	7	18	32	54
6 Walsall	46	12	8	3	35	17	6	9	8	26	33	53
7 Gillingham	46	11	10	2	36	21	4	10	9	31	39	50
8 Colchester	46	10	11	2	36	16	5	7	11	19	28	48
9 Chesterfield	46	14	6	3	40	16	3	8	12	18	33	48
10 Swindon	46	12	7	4	40	22	4	9	10	27	38	48
11 Shrewsbury	46	11	7	5	42	23	5	8	10	21	34	47
12 Tranmere	46	13	7	3	39	19	3	8	12	18	33	47
13 Carlisle	46	10	9	4	32	26	4	10	9	27	33	47
14 Sheffield Wednesday	46	13	7	3	28	14	2	9	12	22	38	46
15 Bury	46	7	13	3	34	22	6	6	11	28	34	45
16 Lincoln City	46	10	8	5	35	26	5	7	11	18	35	45
17 Exeter City	46	11	8	4	30	18	4	6	13	19	41	44
18 Oxford United	46	11	10	2	38	21	2	4	17	26	46	40
19 Plymouth Argyle	46	7	8	8	33	28	4	9	10	28	40	39
20 Rotherham United	46	11	5	7	26	19	2	8	13	25	49	39
21 Port Vale	46	7	11	5	28	23	1	9	13	18	44	36
22 Bradford City	46	11	6	6	40	29	1	4	18	16	57	34
23 Hereford United	46	9	9	5	28	22	0	5	18	6	38	32
24 POMPEY	46	4	11	8	31	38	3	6	14	10	37	31

POMPEY v MANSFIELD TOWN

Pompey joined the Football League in 1920, and Mansfield Town in 1931, yet the two clubs have only been in the same division for one season. Their first league meeting ended in a 2-2 draw at Fratton Park in January 1977, and the Stags won 2-0 at Field Mill later in the season. They were drawn together in the Carling Cup in 2006/07; the only other occasion on which the two clubs met was in a friendly at Field Mill in 1971, that finished 1-1.

THE RESERVES WON TOO!

Whilst Pompey were outplaying Wolves at Wembley to win the FA Cup in 1939, Pompey Reserves beat Tottenham Hotspur's second string 3-0 at White Hart Lane thanks to a second-half hat trick by Jimmy Beattie. Appearing in the Pompey team were Reg Flewin, Phil Rookes, and Bill Hindmarsh, three men who would contribute greatly to the club's double League Championship success a decade later.

TOP FIVE HOME ATTENDANCES

26/02/1949 ....Derby County, FA Cup sixth round 51,385
01/10/1949 ....Wolverhampton Wanderers, Division One 50,248
15/02/1950 ....Manchester United, FA Cup fifth round replay 49,962
24/03/1951 ....Tottenham Hotspur, Division One.........................49,716
12/02/1949 ....Newport County, FA Cup fifth round 48,581

28-YEAR WAIT

Pompey supporters who hoped for a swift return to the First Division after the club was relegated in 1959 would have been very disappointed. It was 28 years before Fratton Park staged Division One football again, and Oxford United and Wimbledon, both non-league clubs at the time Pompey dropped into the Second Division, reached the top flight before Pompey completed their climb back in 1987.

NEW SONG

In 1973, Pompey supporters were invited to enter a competition to write a new song for the club. The winner was Mr. W.M. Benfield, who wrote the following words to the tune *Camptown Races*:

> *Who's the team that plays the best? Pompey! Pompey!*
> *Who's the team to beat the rest? Pompey all the way,*
> *Pompey all the way, Pompey all the way,*
> *We'll cheer our team 'cause they're supreme,*
> *Pompey all the way.*

SIX EVER-PRESENTS

Six members of the Pompey side that achieved promotion to the First Division in 1927 played in every match throughout the campaign. They were: George Clifford, Reg Davies, Harry Foxall, Billy Moffat, Billy Haines, and Freddie Cook.

POMPEY'S FIRST MATCH

Pompey's first competitive match was played at Chatham in the Southern League on 2 September 1899. They won the match 1-0, with the goal being credited to Nobby Clarke, although the ball struck a defender before entering the net.

SUBSTITUTE BARTLETT

Two players with the surname Bartlett have appeared in Pompey's league side, but neither started a match. Gordon Bartlett made two appearances as substitute during the 1974/75 season, and Kevin Bartlett (no relation) came off the bench three times in the 1980/81 campaign.

ONLY FISH IN THE SEA

In 1965, in an effort to cut costs and because of the concern that so few young players were coming up through the ranks and making their mark in Pompey's first team, the club made the drastic decision of abandoning their youth and reserve teams and decided to concentrate solely on an 18-man squad. Manager George Smith made the statement that there were "only fish in the sea around Portsmouth". Ironically, one young player allowed to leave Fratton Park was Mick Mills, who went on to win 42 caps for England, and also captained his country on a few occasions.

THE POMPEY

The Pompey Shop that stands outside Fratton Park on the corner of Frogmore Road and Carisbrooke Road was for many years a public house called 'The Pompey.' The change from pub to club shop was made in 1988.

BUYING A GOALKEEPER

When Pompey paid £200,000 to Swiss club FC Wil for Mart Poom in 1995, it was the first time in 21 years that the club paid a transfer fee for a goalkeeper. David Best was the last keeper bought by the club, from Ipswich Town for £22,500 in February 1974.

LONG-SERVING SECRETARY

Pompey's longest-serving employee is club secretary Paul Weld. He joined the Fratton Park staff in 1973, having spent two years in the Football Association's accounts department. He was promoted to club secretary in 1989.

SOS POMPEY

'SOS Pompey' was the name given to a fundraising campaign launched in September 1976 in an effort to save the club from financial ruin. It was announced that £25,000 was needed by 1 November in order to pay the club's most pressing debts, and when the campaign was wound up in April 1977, over £35,000 had been collected.

A GAMBLE ON REYNOLDS

Manager Ron Tindall admitted to taking a huge gamble when he signed Richard Reynolds from Plymouth Argyle in 1971. He had not seen him play for several years, but had been impressed with his displays in the past when the two had met on opposing sides. The striker responded by playing in all but one of Pompey's matches throughout the 1971/72 season, finishing as top goal-scorer and scooping the club's Player of the Year award.

THEY LET THEM GO

Two players who hold all-time goalscoring records for league clubs began their careers with Pompey. Ray Crawford, a Pompey player in the late 1950s, scored 203 league goals in two spells with Ipswich Town, and John Atyeo, who played twice as an amateur during the 1950/51 season, struck 214 times as well as breaking the league appearance record with 597 for Bristol City.

LAST-DAY SURVIVAL

Pompey saved themselves from relegation on the last day of the season three times in six years. In 1996, a Deon Burton goal was enough to earn Pompey, then managed by Terry Fenwick, an away win at Huddersfield Town, and two years later a brace by John Durnin and another from Sammy Igoe gave Alan Ball's team a 3-1 win against Bradford City at Valley Parade. By 2001, Graham Rix was in charge, and a 3-0 win at home to Barnsley, thanks to goals by Lee Bradbury, Gary O'Neil and Kevin Harper, kept them afloat.

JACK'S FIRST MATCH

Leeds United and England legend Jack Charlton led Middlesbrough to the Second Division championship in 1973/74, his first season as a manager. His first match in charge was against Pompey at Fratton Park on the opening day of the campaign. Boro won 1-0.

BOBBY STOKES

Portsmouth-born Bobby Stokes scored the only goal in the 1976 FA Cup Final as Southampton beat Manchester United at Wembley, but he could well have moved to Fratton Park earlier in the season. It was all set for Pompey's Paul Went to sign for Saints in December 1975, with Stokes coming to Fratton Park as part of the package, but the deal fell through at the last hurdle. Stokes eventually signed for Pompey in August 1977. He died tragically in May 1995, aged 44.

SCOULAR WINS THE CUP

Jimmy Scoular was the only member of Pompey's double championship side to win a major honour with another club. He skippered Newcastle United to FA Cup triumph over Manchester City at Wembley in 1955.

TOP MARKSMEN

Peter Harris 194
Johnny Weddle 173
Ron Saunders 139
Duggie Reid 129
Billy Haines 119
Ray Hiron 110
Johnny Gordon..................................107
Jimmy Easson 103
Guy Whittingham 99
Albert McCann 83

GRAHAM IN TWO SWAP DEALS

George Graham left Fratton Park as he arrived – in a straight swap deal. In November 1974, he signed from Manchester United, with Ron Davies moving to Old Trafford, and two years later he was transferred to Crystal Palace in a swap for David Kemp.

HANDSOME GEORGE

In 1968, Pompey full-back George Ley was voted the most handsome footballer in a poll run by the *Football League Review*, a magazine given free with a matchday programme. With one day to go before the final count, Ley and George Best were joint top with 40,179 votes each, and on the last day, three more votes came through the door, all for the Pompey player.

JIMMY'S RETIREMENT GIFT

Jimmy Dickinson played his 764th and final league match at Northampton on his 40th birthday on 24 April 1965. After the match the Northampton directors presented him with a retirement present – a pair of slippers.

IN THE BASEMENT

Pompey spent two seasons in the Fourth Division. They were relegated to the basement of the Football League in 1978 and, after looking certainties for instant promotion in the first half of the season, they finished in seventh place. The following season they won promotion on the final day, winning 2-0 at Northampton and going up on goal difference.

KEEP IT IN THE FAMILY

In the late 1960s, six former Pompey players held full-time jobs at Fratton Park. Jimmy Dickinson was employed as Public Relations Officer and later secretary – and manager in the 1970s – while his former team-mate of the 1940s and 1950s, Duggie Reid, was the groundsman. Gordon Neave, a former reserve half-back, was head trainer, with Bobby Campbell as his assistant. The others were chief scout Tony Barton, and John McClelland, who worked at the ground as a maintenance man.

DOWN AND BACK

Peter Ellis was the only player to make Pompey's round trip from the Second Division to the Fourth and back again. Making his league debut in Division Two as an 18-year-old in 1974, he suffered two relegations in 1976 and 1978, but played his part in the Pompey revival that saw them return to Division Three in 1980 and the Second Division in 1983. He stayed with the club for one season in Division Two before joining Southend United.

FOUR FOR MIDDLETON

Harry Middleton is the only Pompey player to have scored four goals in a League Cup tie. He achieved the feat on 1 November 1961, in a 4-2 second-round replay win at Derby County.

SENIOR SERVICE

Trevor Senior, who scored more than 150 goals in two spells at Reading, began his league career with Pompey. He scored just two goals while at Fratton Park – both against Reading.

LAST DAY ESCAPE III

3 May 1998, Division One....................................Bradford City 1 Pompey 3

Pompey's fate went to the last game for the second time in three years, and they nearly fell behind after 12 minutes when Nigel Pepper smacked a shot against the Pompey bar. Craig Ramage prodded the rebound against the post. News came through that Manchester City had scored at Stoke, and temporarily Pompey were in the bottom three, but Sammy Igoe forced Gary Walsh into a sliced clearance, and rolled the loose ball into the path of John Durnin to give Pompey the lead. Aaron Flahavan made two fine saves early in the second half before Igoe made it 2-0 with a firm finish. John Durnin then nodded in a third. Ramage netted a late consolation goal for the home side. POMPEY: Aaron Flahavan, Robbie Pethick, Matthew Robinson, David Hillier, Dave Waterman, Andy Awford, Michalis Vlachos, Sammy Igoe, Mathias Svensson, John Durnin, Andy Thomson.

TOP GOALSCORERS IV

Pompey's top league goalscorers between 1976/77 and 1987/88 were:

1976/77	David Kemp	16
1977/78	David Kemp	16
1978/79	Colin Garwood	15
1979/80	Colin Garwood	17
1980/81	David Gregory	13
1981/82	Billy Rafferty	17
1982/83	Alan Biley	23
1983/84	Mark Hateley	22
1984/85	Neil Webb	16
1985/86	Nicky Morgan	14
1986/87	Mick Quinn	22
1987/88	Kevin Dillon	9

JUST MADE IT

On 6 September 1958, after a journey by taxi and aircraft, Gillingham centre-forward Ron Saunders arrived at Fratton Park at 2.20pm to sign for Pompey – just in time to lead the attack against Chelsea. Storm damage and floods had blocked road and rail routes out of Gillingham. Saunders had been unable to reach London to meet Pompey boss Freddie Cox, who had travelled to the capital to complete the transfer. Eventually Saunders and Gills boss Harry Barratt flew to Portsmouth from Croydon. Saunders was unable to claim a debut goal in the 2-2 draw.

EIGHT CONSECUTIVE CLEAN SHEETS

Pompey's longest run of matches without conceding a goal is eight. They began the 1922-23 season with a goalless draw at home to Bristol Rovers, and goalkeeper Tommy Newton was not beaten until the ninth match of the campaign, when Jack Fowler netted at Fratton Park for Plymouth Argyle. The visitors won the match 2-1.

JACK TINN

Jack Tinn, at 20 years, is Pompey's longest-serving manager. He didn't play football seriously, but his ability to spot a player with potential was second to none. After working as a senior clerk for the South Shields County Court, he took over as manager of South Shields in 1919. Following Pompey's promotion to Division One in 1927, he succeeded John McCartney, and quickly went about building a side to make an impact in the top league. He acquired the likes of Jack Smith from his old club South Shields, along with Jimmy Nichol, Johnny Weddle, and Jock Gilfillan, and the team reached the FA Cup Final in 1929, only to be beaten 2-0 by Bolton Wanderers. The team was ever improving, and finished fourth in the First Division in 1930/31, even leading the table briefly in September 1932. The club reached Wembley again in 1934, but were beaten on this occasion 2-1 by Manchester City. Tinn gradually rebuilt the side, and they went top of the League in September 1936, remaining there for four months before finally slipping to ninth. It was third time lucky for Pompey when they beat Wolverhampton Wanderers 4-1 in the 1939 FA Cup Final, which is remembered for Jack Tinn's lucky spats. League football was suspended for seven years due to World War II, so what heights Tinn's young team would have reached will never be known. Tinn resigned in 1947 after managing the club throughout the first post-war Football League season, but left a legacy in the shape of players he signed during the war – the likes of Jimmy Dickinson, Peter Harris, Duggie Reid, Jack Froggatt, Len Phillips, and Jimmy Scoular, all of whom would play a major part in Pompey's success story of the late 1940s and early 1950s.

88 POINTS NOT ENOUGH

Pompey collected 88 points during the 1992/93 season, but it was not enough to achieve automatic promotion. They were beaten to second spot by West Ham United on goal difference, meaning Pompey had to go through the play-offs. Because of alterations to Leicester City's Filbert Street ground, the first leg of the semi-final was played at Nottingham Forest's City Ground. Leicester won the match 1-0, and held the Blues to a 2-2 draw at Fratton Park.

GOING UP

The 1979/80 season saw Pompey climb out of Division Four on goal difference. Promotion looked a certainty early in the season, as the team won ten out of the first 11 games, and continued to win in style, scoring 61 league goals before the turn of the year. They stuttered after Christmas, but a good run of results put them in with a chance as they travelled to Northampton Town on the final day, and a 2-0 Pompey victory, coupled with Bradford City's defeat at Peterborough, put them up on goal difference.

Football League Division Four 1979/80

	Pl	W	D	L	F	A	W	D	L	F	A	Pts
1 Huddersfield Town	46	16	5	2	61	18	11	7	5	40	30	66
2 Walsall	46	12	9	2	43	23	11	9	3	32	24	64
3 Newport County	46	16	5	2	47	22	11	2	10	36	28	61
4 POMPEY	46	15	5	3	62	23	9	7	7	29	26	60
5 Bradford City	46	14	6	3	44	14	10	6	7	33	36	60
6 Wigan Athletic	46	13	5	5	42	26	8	8	7	34	35	55
7 Lincoln City	46	14	8	1	43	12	4	9	10	21	30	53
8 Peterborough	46	14	3	6	39	22	7	7	9	19	25	52
9 Torquay United	46	13	7	3	47	25	2	10	11	23	44	47
10 Aldershot	46	10	7	6	35	23	6	6	11	27	30	45
11 Bournemouth	46	8	9	6	32	25	5	9	9	20	26	44
12 Doncaster Rovers	46	11	6	6	37	27	4	8	11	25	36	44
13 Northampton Town	46	14	5	4	33	16	2	7	14	18	50	44
14 Scunthorpe United	46	11	9	3	37	23	3	6	14	21	52	43
15 Tranmere Rovers	46	10	4	9	32	24	4	9	10	18	32	41
16 Stockport County	46	9	7	7	30	31	5	5	13	18	41	40
17 York City	46	9	6	8	35	34	5	5	13	30	48	39
18 Halifax Town	46	11	9	3	29	20	2	4	17	17	52	39
19 Hartlepool	46	10	7	6	36	28	4	3	16	23	36	38
20 Port Vale	46	8	6	9	34	24	4	6	13	22	46	36
21 Hereford United	46	8	7	8	22	21	3	7	13	16	31	36
22 Darlington	46	7	11	5	33	26	2	6	15	17	48	35
23 Crewe Alexandra	46	10	6	7	25	27	1	7	15	10	41	35
24 Rochdale	46	6	7	10	20	28	1	6	16	13	51	27

CHANNON'S MILESTONE

Mick Channon enjoyed a long football career playing for a number of clubs, most notably Southampton, but it was as a Pompey player that he made his 700th league appearance in November 1985, away to Grimsby Town in the Second Division. Sadly for Mick, the home side won 1-0.

POMPEY'S FIRST CONTINENTAL

Dan Ekner from Sweden was Pompey's first continental player. He came to Portsmouth in 1949 to take up a business studies course, and played five matches as an amateur during Pompey's second League title campaign.

YOUNGEST CAPTAINS

The youngest player to captain Pompey in a senior game was Kit Symons, who was aged 19 when he skippered them in a Zenith Data Systems Cup match against Plymouth Argyle at Home Park. Pompey lost 1-0. The youngest club captain was Paul Cahill, who was aged 21 when he led them throughout the 1976/77 campaign.

ONLY SEVEN MINUTES OF FIRST-TEAM FOOTBALL

Paul Smith played for Pompey for just seven minutes. The midfielder signed for the club on a free transfer from Manchester City in the summer of 1973, and spent a season at Fratton Park. His seven minutes of action came in March 1974, when he was brought on as a substitute in Pompey's 2-1 victory at Swindon.

TALLEST PLAYER

The tallest player to represent Pompey is 6'7" centre forward Peter Crouch. Signed from Queens Park Rangers for £1.25m in 2001, he scored 19 goals in 37 league and cup appearances before being sold the following March to Aston Villa for £5m.

NUMBERED SHIRTS

The first time Pompey wore numbered shirts was on 25 March 1939, when they beat Huddersfield Town 2-1 at Highbury in the FA Cup semi-final. The numbering of shirts became official at the beginning of the 1939/40 season, and Pompey wore shirts with numbers for the first time at Fratton Park on 26 August 1939 in a 2-1 win against Blackburn Rovers.

MOST CONSECUTIVE LEAGUE APPEARANCES

The longest run of consecutive league appearances by a Pompey player is 185 by Jimmy Dickinson. The run began on 4 February 1961 in a 2-0 defeat at Plymouth Argyle in Division Two, and ended on 19 April 1965 as Pompey defeated Norwich City 4-0 at home in another Second Division fixture. This was Dickinson's final match at Fratton Park before his retirement.

JACK TINN'S LUCKY SPATS

Jack Tinn's lucky spats are part of Pompey folklore. Tinn was given a pair of spats as a good luck charm before the third round FA Cup tie against Manchester United at Old Trafford in 1934. Freddie Worrall insisted he strap the spats on to the legs of his boss, and as Pompey drew with United and won the replay, this ritual occurred before every FA Cup tie that the team were involved in.

GUTHRIE REUNITED WITH CUP MEDAL

Jimmy Guthrie, who captained Pompey to their 1939 FA Cup Final triumph, was without his winners' medal for 33 years. In 1940, he lent the medal to a sick friend, but never went back to retrieve it, and as time went by they lost touch. For many years the medal was in the possession of Mrs Netta Tilbury, daughter of former Pompey captain and chairman Bob Blyth, who tried in vain to trace Guthrie. However, in 1973, he attended a reunion of former Pompey players, and was presented with the medal in front of some of his former team-mates.

EITHER SIDE OF THE WAR

Seven players have represented Pompey before and after World War II. A record of their league appearances and goals is set out below.

	Pre-war		Post-war		Total	
	Apps	Gls	Apps	Gls	Apps	Gls
Bert Barlow	14	5	91	27	105	32
Reg Flewin	1	0	152	0	153	0
Jimmy McAlinden	20	4	33	5	53	9
Cliff Parker	173	50	69	7	242	57
Phil Rookes	5	0	109	0	114	0
Harry Walker	38	0	11	0	49	0
Guy Wharton	66	2	18	1	84	3

NEARLY A HAT TRICK FOR GARWOOD

Kevin Dillon is the only player to have scored a hat trick of penalties for Pompey, but Colin Garwood almost beat him to the record. In a Fourth Division fixture with York City at Fratton Park in September 1979, he converted two penalties as Pompey defeated their opponents 5-2. With six minutes to go, he had the chance to make it a trio of spot-kicks, but visiting goalkeeper Joe Neenan produced a spectacular save to deny him his treble.

time, Michael Reddy slotted home the winning goal, so promotion
celebrations were put on hold for three days until a Svetoslav Todorov
goal earned Pompey that priceless win at home to Burnley.

CLUB SECRETARIES

Pompey have only had eight secretaries since being formed in 1898.

Percy Whitney	1899-1907
George Preston	1907-1946
Dan Clarke	1946-1950
Philip Harris	1950-1956
Reg Mulcock	1956-1968
Jimmy Dickinson	1968-1977
Bill Davis	1977-1989
Paul Weld	1989-

STILL WAITING FOR A FINAL

Pompey have not played in a major final since the Second World War.
Their last final appearance was at Wembley in a Wartime Cup Final in 1942,
when they lost 2-0 to Brentford.

MICK BAXTER – A TRAGEDY

Mick Baxter was Alan Ball's first signing when he took over as manager in
1984, but tragically he never played a first-team game. Signed from
Middlesbrough to shore up a defence that had conceded 64 goals from
42 league matches the previous season, he played in one pre-season
friendly, but complained of feeling unwell during a training session. It was
discovered he was suffering from Hodgkin's Disease, and although he
remained on the Fratton payroll for some time, his football career had
come to an end. He died in 1989, aged 32.

FIRST OFF

The first Pompey player sent off was Roderick Walker. He received his
marching orders in a 2-1 home defeat to Bristol Rovers on 7 January 1905.

ONLY PLAYER-MANAGER

The only player-manager Pompey have had in their history is Steve Claridge. Already a player with the club, he combined both roles when Tony Pulis was sacked in October 2000, but after a poor run of results was replaced by Graham Rix in February 2001. Chairman Milan Mandaric wanted Claridge to stay on as a player, but he went on loan to Millwall.

PROUD CUP DISPLAYS

The 1975/76 season saw Pompey finish bottom in Division Two. Their league form was appalling, but they fared well against First Division sides in both cup competitions. They held Leicester City to a 1-1 draw in the first leg of a second round League Cup tie, only to lose to a single goal in the last minute of extra time in the second leg at Filbert Street. In the FA Cup, they beat Birmingham City 1-0 in a third round replay at St Andrews after drawing 1-1 at Fratton Park.

POMPEY'S FIRST LEAGUE MATCH

Pompey won their first Football League match 3-0 at home to Swansea Town in Division Three (South). Frank Stringfellow was captain, in the absence of A.E. Knight. Billy James, Stringfellow and Billy Reid got the goals. The Pompey team was: Ned Robson, Bill Probert, Joe Potts, Shirley Abbott, Jack Harwood, Joe Turner, Ernie Thompson, Frank Stringfellow, Billy Reid, Billy James, Willie Beedie.

PEACEFUL PROTEST

In December 1998, Pompey fans invaded the Fratton Park pitch during the interval of the match with Grimsby Town to protest against chairman Martin Gregory in front of the Sky TV cameras. Grimsby won the match 1-0.

ONLY SIX GOALSCORERS

When Pompey won the First Division Championship in 1949, they scored 84 league goals. Two were own goals, but the other 82 were shared among only six players. They were Peter Harris (18), Duggie Reid (17), Jack Froggatt (15), Ike Clarke (14), Len Phillips (10) and Bert Barlow (8).

BASEBALL AT FRATTON PARK

On 6 June 1918, Fratton Park staged a game of baseball. The USA beat Canada 4-3 in a match held in aid of the Red Cross.

BOBBY MOORE NEARLY JOINED POMPEY

England's 1966 World Cup-winning captain Bobby Moore was very close to becoming a Pompey player. In 1974, chairman John Deacon was first in the race – long before West Ham officially announced they were to part with their skipper and a fee of £25,000 was agreed. Moore seemed certain to sign, but then Fulham stepped in, and he moved to Craven Cottage.

BARNARD DENIED

Pompey midfielder Leigh Barnard was denied a spectacular first league goal by referee Alan Gunn. In a Fourth Division clash with Crewe Alexandra at Fratton Park in September 1978, Barnard let fly from 25 yards and his shot flew into the top corner and bounced out. As the Pompey players congratulated him, Crewe carried on with the play. Mr Gunn thought Barnard's shot had hit the crossbar.

SPECTACULAR OWN GOAL

In 1976, Pompey tried young centre forward Steve Foster at centre-half in a reserve match as "an experiment." So good were his early displays in the position that he was soon promoted to first-team duty for a Third Division clash at home to Bury. He gave a faultless performance… except that he made a spectacular dive to head the ball clear, and only succeeded in powering it into the top corner past his own goalkeeper.

4-1 SCORELINES

Four of Pompey's six opening fixtures of the 1965/66 campaign ended 4-1. They won their first match at home to Plymouth Argyle 4-1, then lost their second game, away to Preston North End, by the same score. They followed that by earning a 2-2 draw at Southampton, but defeated Preston 4-1 in the return fixture at Fratton Park. The next match was lost 2-0 away to Bolton Wanderers, and then they were beaten 4-1 by Crystal Palace at Selhurst Park. Three more matches during the campaign produced the same scoreline.

FASTEST DEBUT GOAL

The fastest goal by a player making his Pompey debut was scored by David Dodson. Three days after signing from Swansea in December 1961, he played at outside-left in a Second Division home fixture against Swindon Town, and headed Pompey into the lead after 19 seconds. The match ended 2-2.

HONOURS WON BY POMPEY

FA Cup 1939
FA Cup Finalists 1929,1934
FA Charity Shield (shared) 1949-50
Western League Champions 1901,1902,1903
Southern League Champions...1902,1920
Southern League Runners-up 1912
Football League Division One Champions..........1948/49,1949/50, 2002/03
Football League Division Two Runners-up.........................1926/27,1986/87
Football League Division Three Champions.....................1961/62, 1982/83
Football League Division Three (South) Champions 1923/24
Hants Charity Cup Winners 1906,1907
South Western League Champions..1916
South Hants War League Champions..1918
Pickford Cup Winners 1914, 1915, 1921, 1924, 1926, 1928, 1931-36
Hants Benevolent Cup Winners 1911
Hospital Cup Winners....................................1924-27, 1929, 1930, 1933-35
Hants Professional Cup Winners 1935,1982
Hants Professional Cup Runners-up...1983
Hants Combination Cup Winners 1933, 1941
Hampshire Football Association Benevolent Fund Cup ......(shared) 1909
London Combination Winners (reserves) 1936
London Midweek League Champions (reserves) 1974, 1977, 1983,1984
London Midweek League Cup Winners (reserves) 1984
Hants League Champions (reserves) 1903, 1904, 1939-40
Hants League Southern Division Champions (reserves).....................1911
Southern Charity Cup Winners..1903
Southern Charity Cup Runners-up...1909
South Western Combination Champions 1916
Southern Professional Floodlight Cup Winners 1958
Southern Floodlit Combination Cup Winners 1958

FIRST PREMIERSHIP MATCH

Pompey's first Premiership fixture was at home to Aston Villa on 16 August 2003, and they won the match 2-1. Teddy Sheringham gave Pompey the lead three minutes before half-time, and Patrik Berger added a second on 63 minutes. Gareth Barry pulled a goal back with a disputed penalty six minutes from time, but Pompey held out for a deserved win. The Pompey team was as follows: Shaka Hislop, Boris Zivkovic, Hayden Foxe, Dejan Stefanovic, Arjan de Zeeuw, Steve Stone, Amdy Faye (Sebastien Schemmel), Nigel Quashie, Patrik Berger, Teddy Sheringham, Yakubu Ayegbeni (Vincent Pericard).

NEW STAND

In October 1997, Pompey opened a new stand behind the Fratton goal, known as the KJC Stand. The cost was £2.5m, and the 4,500 seats raised Fratton Park's capacity to 19,000.

WALKABOUT AT FRATTON

In October 1977, 550 Portsmouth schoolboys and girls walked 20 laps of the Fratton Park pitch to raise money for Portsmouth Football Club and the Portsmouth Schools Football Association. The two beneficiaries each received over £1,000.

UP FOR THE CUP II

FA Cup Final 1934
28 April 1934, Wembley Stadium
MANCHESTER CITY (0)2   *v*   PORTSMOUTH (1) 1
Tilson 2   Rutherford
Attendance 93,258

Five years and one day after losing to Bolton Wanderers, Pompey returned to Wembley to face Manchester City in the FA Cup Final. They took the lead through Sep Rutherford after 27 minutes, but the match turned when centre-half Jimmy Allen was carried off with concussion. Fred Tilson equalised for City, and although Allen returned, he was still dazed, and could do nothing to stop Tilson grabbing the winner for City. POMPEY: Jock Gilfillan, Alex Mackie, Willie Smith, Jimmy Nichol, Jimmy Allen, Dave Thackeray, Fred Worrall, Jack Smith, Johnny Weddle, Jimmy Easson, Freddie Cook.

LUCKY FIRST FOR HARRIS

Peter Harris is Pompey's record league goal-scorer, but he was fortunate with his first goal for the club. Playing in only his second match, against Aldershot in a Wartime League South fixture in 1944, he aimed for the far corner, but the ball sliced off his boot and crept inside the near post.

KELLARD SETS RECORDS

Pompey collected their then-record transfer fee in June 1968, when Bobby Kellard was sold to Bristol City for £35,000, and they paid their then-record fee when they brought him back to Fratton Park from Crystal Palace for £42,000 in December 1972.

TWO FRATTON DEBUTS

Former England captain Gerry Francis made his Football League debut for Queens Park Rangers at Fratton Park in September 1969. He also made his debut for England under-23s at the ground, against Denmark in 1973.

CAPTAIN PHILLIPS

1950s wing-half Johnny Phillips captained every team he played for except the Pompey senior side. As a schoolboy, he captained Portsmouth Primaries and Seniors before leading the Pompey Juniors. He then moved up through the club ranks, skippering Pompey 'B', Pompey 'A' and the reserves, but never led out the first team.

GREAT START

When Pompey beat Millwall 1-0 at Fratton Park on 14 September 2002, it meant Pompey had made their best start to a season. Seven wins and a draw from eight matches eclipsed the start of 1922/23 and 1948/49. They followed the win over the Lions with a 4-1 victory at home to Wimbledon, but suffered their first defeat of the campaign the following week, losing 1-0 away to Norwich City.

THREE DEBUT SCORERS

On the opening day of the 1982/83 campaign, Pompey beat Sheffield United 4-1, and three Pompey players scored on their debuts. Alan Biley equalised in the first half, and after the break Ernie Howe put Pompey in front, with Neil Webb adding a third. The fourth goal was scored by old-stager Mick Tait.

FATHER CHRISTMAS

In December 1984, Pompey beat Oxford United 2-1 at Fratton Park in a top-of-the-table clash. With time running out and Pompey 1-0 down, a fan dressed as Father Christmas ran onto the pitch, and in the time added on for this incident, Alan Biley headed two goals for the Blues. The victory put Pompey in second place, with Oxford dropping to fourth.

NO TO SOUTHAMPTON

In 1952 Reg Flewin turned down the opportunity to manage Southampton. His first managerial appointment came in 1960, when he left his position as assistant manager at Fratton Park to take over at Stockport County.

ROGERS FOUND THE NET MORE EASILY

Alan Rogers scored more goals in his first season with Pompey than he managed in five years with Plymouth Argyle. He struck nine times for Pompey during the 1979/80 campaign, whereas he only found the net on five occasions while with the Pilgrims.

HARRIS KEPT POMPEY UP

A header by Harry Harris on 23 April 1960 kept Pompey in Division Two. He cancelled out a goal by Hull City's Chris Morris in the penultimate match of the season at Fratton Park, and the 1-1 draw meant Pompey stayed up and the Tigers went down.

LET'S START WITH A HAT TRICK

Two Pompey players have scored a hat trick on the opening day of the season. On 18 August 1962, David Dodson scored three times in a 4-1 home win over Walsall in Division Two, and Guy Whittingham grabbed a hat trick on 15 August 1992, in a 3-3 draw in a First Division fixture at Bristol City.

STIRRING THE BLOOD

A free day for the players was introduced by George Smith soon after his appointment as manager in 1961. It was designed to enable the individual to develop and improve his own skill, and to practise the aspect of his play that he felt needed extra attention. Thursday was the day for 'stirring the blood,' the day the players were extended to the peak of their fitness.

WIN AT MOLINEUX

In January 1997, Pompey won at Molineux for the first time since 1951, beating Wolverhampton Wanderers 2-1 in the FA Cup third round with headed goals by Alan McLoughlin and Paul Hall. They made it a double on the final day of the League season, winning again at Molineux 1-0, Hall finding the net again.

LET'S SWITCH GROUNDS

Requesting to play a home FA Cup tie on the opponent's ground is not a new idea. In 1904, Chesterfield were drawn to play Pompey at their Saltergate home, but chose to play the tie at Fratton Park. The match finished 0-0, and Pompey won the replay 2-0 at Fratton Park four days later.

GOING UP II

Pompey ended the 1982/83 season as champions of Division Three after spending seven years in football's lower reaches. They won nine consecutive home matches, and also won a club record seven successive victories. Promotion was clinched as Pompey beat Southend United 2-0 at Fratton Park on 7 May 1983, and the title was won a week later at Plymouth, where an Alan Biley goal was enough to secure victory.

Football League Division Three 1982/83

	Pl	W	D	L	F	A	W	D	L	F	A	Pts
1 POMPEY	46	16	4	3	43	19	11	6	6	31	22	91
2 Cardiff City	46	17	5	1	45	14	8	6	9	31	36	86
3 Huddersfield Town	46	15	8	0	56	18	8	5	10	28	31	82
4 Newport County	46	13	7	3	40	20	10	2	11	36	34	78
5 Oxford United	46	12	9	2	41	23	10	3	10	30	30	78
6 Lincoln City	46	17	1	5	55	22	6	6	11	22	29	76
7 Bristol Rovers	46	16	4	3	55	21	6	5	12	29	37	75
8 Plymouth Argyle	46	15	2	6	37	23	4	6	13	24	43	65
9 Brentford	46	14	4	5	50	28	4	6	13	38	49	64
10 Walsall	46	14	5	4	38	19	3	8	12	26	44	64
11 Sheffield United	46	16	3	4	44	20	3	4	16	18	44	64
12 Bradford City	46	11	7	5	41	27	5	6	12	27	42	61
13 Gillingham	46	12	4	7	37	29	4	9	10	21	30	61
14 Bournemouth	46	11	7	5	35	20	5	6	12	24	48	61
15 Southend United	46	10	8	5	41	28	5	6	12	25	37	59
16 Preston North End	46	11	10	2	35	17	4	3	16	25	52	58
17 Millwall	46	12	7	4	41	24	2	6	15	23	53	55
18 Wigan Athletic	46	10	4	9	35	33	5	5	13	25	39	54
19 Exeter City	46	12	4	7	49	43	2	8	13	32	61	54
20 Orient	46	10	6	7	44	38	5	3	15	20	50	54
21 Reading	46	10	8	5	37	28	2	9	12	27	51	53
22 Wrexham	46	11	6	6	40	26	1	9	13	16	50	51
23 Doncaster	46	6	8	9	38	44	3	3	17	19	53	38
24 Chesterfield	46	6	6	11	28	28	2	7	14	15	40	37

POMPEY SET GROUND RECORD

Before Scunthorpe United moved to Glanford Park in 1988, their home was the Old Showground. The visit of Pompey in the FA Cup fourth round on 30 January 1954 set a ground record of 23,935 that was never beaten. The match finished 1-1, and Scunthorpe then forced a 2-2 draw at Fratton Park, but Pompey won 4-0 at Highbury in the second replay.

KNIGHT RUNS THE LINE

In February 1931, the appointed referee failed to turn up to officiate Pompey's First Division clash at home to Everton so A.E. Knight took over as one of the linesmen. He generously donated his match fee to the local Royal Hospital.

'POMPEY' WATCHED POMPEY

Pompey and England outside-right Peter Harris' first wedding anniversary present to his wife Sylvia was a pet poodle. The couple named the dog 'Pompey', and Mrs Harris would take him along to Fratton Park to watch her husband in action.

POMPEY CRICKETERS

John Atyeo	Wiltshire 1950-51
Mike Barnard	Hampshire 1952-56
Charles Burgess Fry	Hampshire, Sussex, England 1892-1911
Stanley Shute Harris	Surrey, Gloucestershire, Sussex 1900-06
Arthur Egerton Knight	Hampshire 1913-23
Arthur Mounteney	Leicestershire 1911-24
Scot Symon	Perthshire, Hampshire 1935-38
Jim Standen	Worcestershire 1965-72
Ron Tindall	Surrey 1956-66
George Wheldon	Worcestershire, Carmarthenshire 1899-1910

'PLUM THE CARTOONIST'

Alexander Plummer was a Portsmouth-based artist who drew something like 20,000 cartoons in a working life of 70 years. He was best known for his brilliant cartoons relating to Portsmouth Football Club, and his offerings of the ups and downs of life at Fratton Park were featured in the local paper *The Football Mail* from 1920 until 1971. He was born on 9 September 1899 – the day Fratton Park staged Pompey's first home league match – and died on Christmas Day 1987.

HAT TRICKS AGAINST THEIR FUTURE CLUB

Ron Davies and John Lathan both scored hat tricks against Pompey and later joined them. Davies scored all three goals in Norwich City's 3-0 win at Fratton Park in December 1965, and Lathan a treble for Sunderland as they defeated Pompey 3-2 at Roker Park in March 1972.

FOUR OR MORE GOALS IN A MATCH

Players who have scored hat tricks for Pompey are too many to mention, but below is a list of players to have scored four or more goals in a competitive game since Pompey entered the Football League in 1920:

5..Alf Strange ....20/01/1923 5-1 v Gillingham..Division Three(South)
5..Peter Harris ....03/09/1958 5-2 v Aston Villa ....Division One
4..Harry Havelock ....20/03/1926 5-1 v Nottingham Forest ....Division Two
4..Billy Haines ....07/05/1927 5-1 v Preston North End ....Division Two
4..Peter Harris ....09/10/1954 6-2 v Sheffield United ....Division One
4..Harry Middleton ......01/11/1961 4-2 v Derby County............................LC 2
4..Ray Hiron ....12/04/1969 5-2 v Norwich City ....Division Two
4..Guy Whittingham ....26/01/1991 5-1 v Bournemouth ....FAC 4
4..Guy Whittingham ....26/12/1992 4-1 v Bristol Rovers ....Division One
4..Yakubu Ayegbeni......15/05/2004 5-1 v Middlesbrough ....Premiership

FIRST £10m PLAYER

When Alan Ball was manager of Exeter City, he predicted one of his players, Martin Phillips, would be Britain's first £10m player. Fortunately for Pompey, when Ball signed him from the Devon club in August 1998, he only cost £100,000. Phillips made a spectacular debut, coming on as substitute as Pompey were leading Queens Park Rangers 1-0 at Fratton Park in a First Division clash. He set up a goal for Alan McLoughlin three minutes from time, and then scored Pompey's third goal in the last minute.

LOWEST GATE FOR SENIOR GAME

The lowest Fratton Park attendance for a first-class fixture is 2,731 when Pompey met Blackburn Rovers in the League Cup second round second leg on 26 September 2000, It finished 1-1. Supporters could have been excused for their lack of interest, as Blackburn won 4-0 at Ewood Park in the first leg.

POMPEY GIVE BLACKBURN A HAND

Blackburn Rovers had scored in every match of the season before they drew 2-2 at Fratton Park in a Second Division fixture on 1 December 1984, but they had to rely on Pompey to keep the run going. Early on, the ball rebounded in off Noel Blake after hitting the post, then Mick Tait sliced the ball out of Alan Knight's hands to give Rovers a 2-0 half-time lead. Kevin Dillon pulled a goal back from the penalty spot before Vince Hilaire crowned his Pompey debut by equalising with a spectacular diving header.

FIRST £1M SALE

The first player to leave Pompey for £1m was Mark Hateley in June 1984, when he signed for AC Milan. He had impressed Pompey a year earlier when he played in an England under-21 international at Fratton Park, and they paid Coventry City £190,000 to bring him to the south coast. He played 38 matches in the Second Division side, and topped the goalscoring charts with 22 league goals. After making four appearances for the full England side at the end of the season, it was inevitable that he would join a major club.

SMITH WAS PLAYER-MANAGER

Jim Smith was player-manager of non-league Boston United when Pompey beat them 1-0 in an FA Cup third round tie in January 1972. It was Smith who headed only partially clear after a free-kick, and Nick Jennings was on hand to curl in the winner.

A POINT LOST

Pompey found points hard to come by throughout the 1975/76 season, and with a minute to go at Notts County, they thought they had done enough to earn one. But Paul Went was adjudged to have fouled Les Bradd in the penalty area, and John Scanlon buried the spot-kick. There was hardly time to re-start… but Eric Probert still found time to add another goal for Notts County.

IGOE THE SUPER SUB

Sammy Igoe has appeared more times as a substitute for Pompey than any other player. He made his league debut when he came off the bench during the final match of the 1994/95 season, when Pompey drew 1-1 with Oldham Athletic at Fratton Park. His last substitute appearance came on 1 March 2000, in a 2-1 defeat at home to Tranmere Rovers, shortly before his transfer to Reading. This was the 68th time Igoe had played as a substitute.

TOP FA CUP GOALSCORER

Peter Harris holds the record for scoring the most goals for Pompey in the FA Cup. He hit 15 goals during a career that spanned 13 years – 1946 to 1959 –his first in the competition coming in a 4-1 win at home to Brighton and Hove Albion in January 1948. His best effort in one season was five in 1948/49, which included a hat-trick at Fratton Park when Pompey thrashed Stockport County 7-0.

POMPEY FOR NORTHERN IRELAND

The following Pompey players have represented Northern Ireland:

Colin Clarke...13
Norman Uprichard..............................13
Jimmy McAlinden 3
Tommy Casey 2
Derek Dougan 1

YOUNG GUN

Jimmy Brown, who helped Pompey gain promotion to the Third Division as a loan player during the 1979/80 campaign, was the youngest player to turn out for Aston Villa. He was 15 years 349 days when Villa lost 2-1 away to Bolton Wanderers in a Second Division fixture on 17 September 1969.

LUCKY THIRTEEN

Pompey made it lucky 13 at Selhurst Park on 18 January 1997, when they finally beat Crystal Palace. Since winning 2-0 against Palace, thanks to goals by Ray Hiron and Albert McCann in December 1966, it took Pompey another 31 years and 13 attempts before they repeated the feat. Pompey looked to be heading for another defeat when Robert Quinn put the Eagles ahead on the half-hour mark, but Lee Bradbury equalised and Andy Thomson struck the winner.

TEN MEN HIT BACK

Ten-man Pompey pulled off a remarkable victory at Huddersfield Town on 15 March 1997. David Hillier was sent off midway through the first half and when Marcus Stewart broke the deadlock, things looked grim for Pompey. However three goals in a four-minute spell during the second half handed Pompey three points. Sammy Igoe levelled for the Blues, then Paul Hall scored twice to complete an amazing comeback and 3-1 victory.

HIGH FIVES II

Two players who have played for Pompey have scored five goals in one match for another club. Ralph Hoten scored five goals for Northampton Town against Crystal Palace in Division Three (South) on 27 October 1928, while Ray Pointer netted five times for Bury in a Second Division fixture against Rotherham United on 2 October 1965.

HEIGHT ADVANTAGE

Pompey centre-half Tommy Rowe, who stood at 6'1", was the tallest player in the 1939 FA Cup Final.

MOST GOALS IN A SEASON

The following former or future Pompey players have top scored for another club:

David Crown ......Southend United 1985/86 24
Ralph Hunt ....Norwich City 1955/56..........................31
Brian Yeo ....Gillingham 1973/74 31

HARRY HARRIS

Harry Harris served Pompey from 1958 to 1971, playing in three divisions as an inside-forward, midfield player and central defender. He began his league career with Newport County, and left the Welsh club for Pompey in July 1958 for a fee of £8,000, plus £2,000 when he had completed 15 appearances. His first season at Fratton Park ended with Pompey losing their First Division status after 32 years, but Harris always played with 100% commitment, and scored 13 goals. He continued to hustle and bustle in Division Two, and his goal against Hull City on the penultimate day of the 1959/60 campaign earned the point that saved the club from a second successive relegation. He later settled into the centre of defence, and was ever-present throughout the 1964/65 campaign. When Jimmy Dickinson retired at the end of the season, Harris took over the club captaincy. In 1970, he rejoined Newport County on loan, making 17 appearances for the Welshmen, but made a sentimental farewell to Hampshire on 1 May 1971, the final day of the 1970/71 season, when, at the age of 37, he captained Pompey in their 2-1 defeat by Second Division champions Leicester City.

HISLOP SETS TRANSFER RECORD

Shaka Hislop, who kept goal for Pompey from 2002 to 2005, brought in Reading's record transfer fee of £1,750,000 when he moved to Newcastle United in August 1995.

MOST GOALS CONCEDED

The most goals Pompey have conceded in one season is 112 in 1958/59. Not surprisingly, the season ended in relegation from the First Division.

ARMFIELD'S FIRST GAME

Former England right-back Jimmy Armfield made a record 568 league appearances for Blackpool between 1954 and 1971. His made his debut on 27 December 1954, at Fratton Park in a First Division fixture against Pompey, who beat the Tangerines 3-0.

BEATING THE CHAMPIONS

When Pompey beat Manchester United 1-0 at Fratton Park on 17 April 2004, it was the first occasion they had beaten the reigning Football League Champions – coincidentally Manchester United – since 19 October 1957.

19 October 1957
MANCHESTER UNITED 0   *v*   POMPEY 3
Henderson, Newman, Harris

MANCHESTER UNITED: Ray Wood, Bill Foulkes, Mark Jones, Eddie Colman, Jackie Blanchflower, Wilf McGuinness, Johnny Berry, Liam Whelan, Alex Dawson, Dennis Viollet, David Pegg.

POMPEY: Norman Uprichard, Phil Gunter, Alex Wilson, Bill Albury, Cyril Rutter, Jimmy Dickinson, Peter Harris, Johnny Gordon, Derek Dougan, Jackie Henderson, Ron Newman.

17 April 2004
POMPEY 1   *v*   MANCHESTER UNITED 0
Stone

POMPEY: Shaka Hislop, Linvoy Primus, Arjan de Zeeuw, Dejan Stefanovic, Matt Taylor, Alexei Smertin, Amdy Faye, Steve Stone, Eyal Berkovic (Nigel Quashie) Lomana LuaLua (Teddy Sheringham), Yakubu.

UNITED: Roy Carroll, Gary Neville, Wes Brown, Mikael Silvestre, John O'Shea (Darren Fletcher), Paul Scholes, Eric Djemba-Djemba (Ronaldo), Nicky Butt (David Bellion), Ole Gunnar Solskjaer, Ryan Giggs, Louis Saha.

FIRST EVER-PRESENT

The first player to feature in every match in an entire season was goalkeeper Tom Cope, who played in all 42 Southern League matches and four FA Cup games throughout the 1909/10 campaign. Cope missed just one match the following season, but the club finished bottom of the Southern League Division One and were relegated.

GOING UP III

Pompey finally returned to the First Division after 28 years. They were unbeaten at home until 20 April when Plymouth Argyle won 1-0. Alan Knight and Kenny Swain were the only two ever-presents, and Mick Quinn was the leading goal-scorer with 22 league goals. The average home league attendance was 13,401.

Football League Division Two 1986/87

	Pl	W	D	L	F	A	W	D	L	F	A	Pts
1 Derby County	42	14	6	1	42	18	11	3	7	22	20	84
2 POMPEY	42	17	2	2	37	11	6	7	8	16	17	78
3 Oldham Athletic	42	13	6	2	36	16	9	3	9	29	28	75
4 Leeds United	42	15	4	2	43	16	4	7	10	15	28	68
5 Ipswich Town	42	12	6	3	29	10	5	7	9	30	33	64
6 Crystal Palace	42	12	4	5	35	20	7	1	13	16	33	62
7 Plymouth Argyle	42	12	6	3	40	23	4	7	10	22	34	61
8 Stoke Ciy	42	11	5	5	40	21	5	5	11	23	32	58
9 Sheffield United	42	10	8	3	31	19	5	5	11	19	30	58
10 Bradford City	42	10	5	6	36	27	5	5	11	26	35	55
11 Barnsley	42	8	7	6	26	23	6	6	9	23	29	55
12 Blackburn Rovers	42	11	4	6	30	22	4	6	11	15	33	55
13 Reading	42	11	4	6	33	23	3	7	11	19	36	53
14 Hull City	42	10	6	5	25	22	3	8	10	16	33	53
15 West Bromwich Albion	42	8	6	7	29	22	5	6	10	22	27	51
16 Millwall	42	10	5	6	27	16	4	4	13	12	29	51
17 Huddersfield Town	42	9	6	6	38	30	4	6	11	16	31	51
18 Shrewsbury Town	42	11	3	7	24	14	4	3	14	17	39	51
19 Birmingham City	42	8	9	4	27	21	3	8	10	20	38	50
20 Sunderland	42	8	6	7	25	23	4	6	11	24	36	48
21 Grimsby Town	42	5	8	8	18	21	5	6	10	21	38	44
22 Brighton & Hove A	42	7	6	8	22	20	2	6	13	15	34	39

FRATTON FACELIFT

Almost immediately after Jim Gregory took charge of the club in 1988, work began to revamp Fratton Park. The top tier of the Fratton stand came down, and the cladding on the North and South stands was replaced, while a new boardroom and dressing rooms were constructed. The contractors faced a tight deadline, having to complete the work by the start of the season, and they almost managed it. There was still work to be done on the South Stand when Leicester City visited Fratton Park on 29 August, so only part of the stand was open to the public.

ONE OUT OF TWO

John Ruggiero took two penalties whilst on loan from Brighton in December 1977. He scored in a 2-2 draw against Cambridge United, and missed in a 3-1 home victory over Bradford City.

MORGAN'S GREAT START

At the start of the 1985/86 season, Nicky Morgan set a new club record by scoring in each of the first five games of the season. His brace at home to Norwich City at Fratton Park in the fifth match earned Pompey a 2-0 win that kept them top of Division Two, and took his tally to seven.

DEATH OF 'BEDDY'

One of Pompey's earliest star players died under tragic circumstances. Centre-forward Frank Bedingfield, affectionately known as Beddy, had been under medical treatment prior to Pompey's FA Cup third round tie at Reading in February 1902, but that didn't stop him from declaring himself fit to play. He collapsed in the dressing-room after scoring the only goal in the match, and consumption was diagnosed. A public fund raised £500 to send him to South Africa in the hope that he would recover, but tragically he died there in 1904 at the age of 27.

BAD BAIRD

Ian Baird is the only player to be sent off at Fratton Park both for and against Pompey. He was ordered off against Charlton Athletic in September 1987 soon after his transfer from Leeds United, and in September 1988, while playing for Leeds in his second spell with them, he was once again sent to the dressing-room.

DEBUT HAT-TRICK

No Pompey man has managed to score a hat trick on his debut, but an opposing player achieved the feat. On 25 March 1967, 19-year-old Colin Viljoen scored three times for Ipswich Town in their 4-2 win over Pompey in a Second Division clash at Portman Road.

FIRST INTERNATIONALS

The match between Ireland and England in Dublin on 17 March 1900 included Pompey's first internationals. Danny Cunliffe turned out at inside-right for England, and Matt Reilly kept goal for Ireland, who won 2-0.

WARTIME SCORELINES

Pompey's biggest victory during World War 2 was 16-1 at home to Clapton Orient on 28 February 1943. Andy Black scored eight of the goals. Other big victories during the war were:

25/01/1941 ....Pompey 10 Bournemouth 2
10/05/1941 ....Pompey 10 Aldershot 2
21/03/1942 ....Pompey 9 Fulham 1
26/12/1945 ....Pompey 9 Crystal Palace 1
08/03/1941 ....Pompey 9 Luton Town 2

FRIENDLY WITH BRIGHTON

A friendly was staged at Fratton Park between Pompey and top-division Brighton and Hove Albion, two days after promotion to the Third Division was attained in May 1980. Jimmy Brown scored the only goal for Pompey, and the match was watched by 14,346.

PARKER MAKES 'EM

Veteran outside-left Cliff Parker was recalled to the Pompey side for the FA Cup fourth round tie against Grimsby Town at Fratton Park in 1950. Pompey won 5-0 and Parker set up four of the goals.

JOE FAGAN GUESTED FOR POMPEY

Joe Fagan, who managed Liverpool from 1983 to 1985, once guested for Pompey during World War II. While on Manchester City's books, he played at centre-half in the game against Clapton Orient at Brisbane Road in a League South fixture that Pompey lost 3-2.

GORDON – THE FIRST PRODIGAL SON

Johnny Gordon was the first Pompey player to return to the club after being transferred. He left for Birmingham City for £15,000 in September 1958 after making 220 appearances for Pompey. He scored 40 goals in 115 appearances for Birmingham City, and when Pompey made it clear in March 1961 they wanted him to return, he turned down offers from Stoke City and Blackpool to come back to Fratton Park. The team were on the brink of relegation to Division Three, but the following year he helped them to the Third Division title in his first full season back with his local club. He clocked up 266 appearances in his second spell with the club, and decided to quit the professional game when he was released in 1967 at the age of 35.

ALEX WILSON

Alex Wilson was born in Buckie, and hadn't been out of Scotland before December 1948, when he travelled down to Portsmouth as a 15-year-old to sign for the club. He made 380 appearances in all competitions between 1951 and 1967, scoring five goals. One of them came in the final match of the 1964/65 season at Northampton, and kept Pompey in the Second Division.

FA CUP WIN AT LAST

When Pompey defeated London Caledonians 5-1 in the FA Cup first round in December 1923, it was the first time they'd won a match in the competition since Bristol Rovers were beaten 2-1 in January 1912.

WHEN POMPEY OUT-SANG THE KOP

Around 12,000 Pompey fans travelled to Anfield on 28 October 1980 to watch the team take on Liverpool in the fourth round of the Football League Cup. They out-sang the famous Liverpool Kop choir throughout the match as Pompey, then a Third Division side, produced a memorable performance. Kenny Dalglish gave Liverpool the lead on 22 minutes, but Alan Kennedy then put through his own goal 14 minutes later for the equaliser. David Johnson gave Liverpool a 2-1 half-time lead and Pompey spent all the second half going for an equaliser, only for Johnson to score Liverpool's third with just ten minutes to play. Graeme Souness volleyed home the fourth in the last minute.

POMPEY'S FIRST MATCH IN EUROPE

Pompey's first European match took place in November 1992. Over 250 fans travelled to Italy to see the 3-0 Anglo-Italian Cup defeat to Bari. The San Nicola Stadium held 60,000 but there were only 837 at the game.

HAVING A LAUGH

Pompey manager Jack Tinn was eager that his players be relaxed before the 1939 FA Cup Final with Wolverhampton Wanderers, so he invited comedian Albert Burden to entertain the players in the dressing-room.

LEAGUE CUP LEGENDS

Albert McCann and Ron Saunders top the list of Pompey League Cup goalscorers with eight apiece.

MR PORTSMOUTH FOOTBALL CLUB

Pompey fanatic John Anthony Westwood is one of the club's best known supporters. In 1989 he changed his name to John Anthony Portsmouth Football Club Westwood.

LONGEST RUN OF LEAGUE DEFEATS

Pompey's longest sequence of league defeats is nine. They were thrashed 6-1 at Old Trafford by Manchester United in the First Division on 27 March 1959, and lost all the remaining matches of the season, ending with a 5-2 defeat by Arsenal at Highbury on 25 April. They also lost nine in a row during the 1975/76 season. The run started at Fratton Park on 21 October, when they were beaten 2-1 by Bristol Rovers in Division Two, and ended on 6 December at the Hawthorns, where West Bromwich Albion beat them 3-1. The next week brought a welcome 1-0 win at Nottingham Forest.

THORNEYCROFTS PLAY AT FRATTON

On 10 January 1920, Fratton Park staged an FA Cup first round tie between Hampshire League side Thorneycrofts and First Division Burnley. The result was 0-0, and Burnley won 5-0 in the replay.

SQUAD NUMBER RETIRED

Before the start of the 2001/02 season, Aaron Flahavan was given number one as his squad number. After he was killed in a car accident a week before the season began, the club retired the squad number in his memory.

IT'S FOUR OUT OF FIVE FOR NIGEL

Nigel Quashie has played for five different clubs in the Premiership, and it is only Pompey with whom he hasn't been relegated. He went down with Queens Park Rangers in 1996, Nottingham Forest in 1999, Southampton in 2005, and West Bromwich Albion in 2006.

POMPEY'S SCHOOLBOY

Pat Neil played nine matches in Pompey's First Division side in 1956 while he was still at school. Aged 17, he was a student at Portsmouth Northern Grammar School, and with no reserve-team experience was drafted into the first team for the season's opening fixture at Huddersfield Town. He played a further eight games, scoring three goals, before being given a well-deserved rest and put in the reserve side.

CUP SHOCK

Pompey produced an FA Cup shock on 15 February 1997, when they beat Premiership Leeds United 3-2 at Elland Road in the fifth round. Alan McLoughlin put Pompey ahead, Lee Bowyer equalised, and Matt Svensson and Lee Bradbury wrapped it up for Pompey. Bowyer struck a second Leeds goal in the dying seconds.

WEAKENED SIDE WINS 5-1

Pompey fielded a much-weakened side, making seven changes, for a League Cup second round tie away to Brighton and Hove Albion in September 1962, but won 5-1. The team was: John Milkins, Phil Gunter, Alfie Noakes, Bobby Campbell, Brian Snowdon, Harry Harris, Tony Barton, Keith Blackburn, Ron Saunders, Roy Smith, David Dodson. The Pompey goalscorers were Ron Saunders (3), and Roy Smith (2).

THE CHAIRMAN BOUGHT HAZARD

Chairman Jim Gregory bought Micky Hazard for Pompey in January 1990 while the club were without a manager. John Gregory had recently been sacked, and Mr Gregory paid Chelsea £100,000 before he handed the manager's job to Frank Burrows.

STARTING EARLY

John Milkins was always going to be a goalkeeper. When he was five years old, his father put up two posts and a rope crossbar on a plot of land next to the family home in Dagenham, Essex.

FLOODLIGHT BREAKTHROUGH

Pompey made history on 7 January 1956 when they played a third round FA Cup tie under floodlights at Fratton Park, beating Grimsby Town 3-1. Four other ties were played under lights that day – the first time the FA had permitted artificial lights at that stage of the competition. A few weeks later, on 22 February, Pompey were the first club to stage a league match under floodlights, when Newcastle United came to Fratton Park and won 2-0.

THREE ON ONE DAY

In January 2006, Pompey signed three players from one club on the same day. Pedro Mendes, Sean Davis, and Noe Pamarot joined from Tottenham Hotspur for a combined fee of £7.5m.

MOST CONSECUTIVE INTERNATIONALS

The most consecutive international appearances made by a Pompey player is 25 by Jimmy Dickinson. He began the run by playing in a 1-1 draw in Cardiff against Wales on 20 October 1951, and appeared in his 25th consecutive international match when England were beaten 4-2 by Uruguay in the 1954 World Cup.

TREBS' EARLY GAMES

Record signing Mike Trebilcock made his Pompey debut away to Rotherham United in February 1968. Albert McCann followed up to score after Trebilcock's shot hit the crossbar. Three minutes into his home debut, Trebilcock scored against Derby County in a 3-2 victory.

TWO ROUND THE WORLD YACHTSMEN

Two Round The World sailors have been guests of honour at Fratton Park. In August 1968, Sir Alec Rose saw Pompey win their first home match of the season 3-0 against Middlesbrough, and in August 1971, Sir Chay Blyth watched a 2-1 victory, again against Middlesbrough, on the opening day of the season.

SEMI-FINAL HEARTACHE

The most shattering blow during Pompey's League Championship-winning season of 1948/49 was undoubtedly the FA Cup semi-final defeat by Leicester City at Highbury. Pompey were almost home and dry as champions, and they only had to beat Leicester City – a struggling Second Division club – to reach Wembley, and possibly be the first club of the 20th century to win the League and Cup double. Pompey started the game well, but fell behind to a Don Revie goal after 15 minutes. Peter Harris levelled for Pompey, but Ken Chisholm netted a second goal for Leicester before half-time. It was clearly not Pompey's day – Harris missed a sitter from six yards, and the match was wrapped up for Leicester when Revie scored a third.

FIRST WIN AT MOLINEUX

Molineux has not been the happiest of venues for Pompey, but they enjoyed their first visit there in February 1925. They beat Wolverhampton Wanderers 5-0, with Billy Haines scoring a hat trick in the last six minutes. This created an away record for the club, and the five-goal margin has still never been bettered in an away fixture.

McLOUGHLIN THE IRISH HERO

Alan McLoughlin scored the goal that put the Republic of Ireland in the 1994 World Cup Finals. Six minutes after coming on as substitute against Northern Ireland at Windsor Park, with the Republic 1-0 down, he sent a curling shot into the net to send his national side to the U.S.A.

RECORD FEE FOR DALE

In July 1951, Pompey paid Chesterfield a £20,000 fee for outside-left Gordon Dale – a record at the time for both clubs. Dale only played in eight matches during his first season at the club because of a series of niggling injuries. It was not until the 1954/55 campaign that he played in more than half the team's league fixtures. During his time at Fratton Park he gave both pleasure and frustration, for he had an extremely individualistic style which supporters either loved or hated. He appeared to adopt a lazy approach, but this was his most dangerous weapon – he would suddenly burst into action, use great ball control, produce a body swerve, and deliver a telling cross. On his day, he was as good as any player in his position in the country, but he couldn't always produce this magical form, and spent a lot of time in the reserves. His presence would put hundreds, if not thousands, on the reserve attendances. In October 1957, he was transferred to Exeter City.

POMPEY'S WAR HERO

Tommy Rowe, who died on 8 May 2006 aged 92, was the last surviving member of Pompey's 1939 FA Cup winning team. He played in the final at centre-half, a position he had made his own since September 1937. When war broke out in 1939, Rowe volunteered to join the Portsmouth City Police, and two years later, became a Royal Air Force bomber pilot. In 1943, he was awarded the Distinguished Flying Cross, and in March 1944, on his 40th mission over Germany, his plane was shot down. He parachuted to relative safety north of Frankfurt, but was a prisoner of war until hostilities ceased. He returned to captain Dorchester, and became their manager in 1953 after a fractured skull ended his playing days.

GAYDAMAK CHEERS PUPILS

A Portsmouth school party were turned away from the Czech Republic v Ghana game in the 2006 World Cup because they fell victim to a ticket scam. When Pompey's joint-owner Sacha Gaydamak heard of their plight, he arranged for tickets to be made available for a new match and paid for their flights to Germany.

HALL'S LAST MATCH

On 21 March 1959, Pompey drew 1-1 at home to Birmingham City – but the visitors' defender Jeff Hall was unknowingly playing his last match. Three days later, Hall was taken critically ill, and died on Saturday 4 April. A minute's silence for the player was held at Fratton Park that afternoon before the First Division match between Pompey and Preston North End.

GOING DOWN IV

Pompey's first campaign back in the First Division, in 1987/88, ended in relegation. Only one point from the first four matches, including a 6-0 thrashing at Arsenal, was not the best start, and by Christmas, a return to the Second Division looked inevitable. A five-match unbeaten run, beginning with a 2-0 win over Southampton at The Dell, lifted them up the table, but after losing 2-0 at home to Liverpool at the end of February, they slipped back into the relegation mire, and their fate was finally sealed away at Coventry City where a disputed penalty, converted by Brian Kilcline, consigned them to the drop.

Football League Division One 1987/88

	Pl	W	D	L	F	A	W	D	L	F	A	Pts
1 Liverpool	40	15	5	0	49	9	11	7	2	38	15	90
2 Manchester United	40	14	5	1	41	17	9	7	4	30	21	81
3 Nottingham Forest	40	11	7	2	40	17	9	6	5	27	22	73
4 Everton	40	14	4	2	34	11	5	9	6	19	16	70
5 Queens Park Rangers	40	12	4	4	30	14	7	6	7	18	24	67
6 Arsenal	40	11	4	5	35	16	7	8	5	23	23	66
7 Wimbledon	40	8	9	3	32	20	6	6	8	26	27	57
8 Newcastle United	40	9	6	5	32	23	5	8	7	23	30	56
9 Luton Town	40	11	6	3	40	21	3	5	12	17	37	53
10 Coventry City	40	6	8	6	23	25	7	6	7	23	28	53
11 Sheffield Wednesday	40	10	2	8	27	30	5	6	9	25	36	53
12 Southampton	40	6	8	6	27	26	6	6	8	22	27	50
13 Tottenham Hotspur	40	9	5	6	26	23	3	6	11	12	25	47
14 Norwich City	40	7	5	8	26	26	5	4	11	14	26	45
15 Derby County	40	6	7	7	18	17	4	6	10	17	28	43
16 West Ham United	40	6	9	5	23	21	3	6	11	17	31	42
17 Charlton Athletic	40	7	7	6	23	21	2	8	10	15	31	42
18 Chelsea	40	7	11	2	24	17	2	4	14	26	51	42
19 POMPEY	40	4	8	8	21	27	3	6	11	15	39	35
20 Watford	40	4	5	11	15	24	3	6	11	12	27	32
21 Oxford United	40	5	7	8	24	34	1	6	13	20	46	31

FA CUP SUPER SUB

Nicky Morgan was the first Pompey substitute to score a goal in the FA Cup. His effort gave Pompey a 2-1 win at home to Grimsby Town in the third round in January 1984.

HIGHEST SOUTHERN LEAGUE ATTENDANCE

The highest attendance at Fratton Park for a Southern League game was the 24,606 people who attended on 3 April 1920. The match with Cardiff City ended in a goalless draw.

FIRST LEAGUE CUP TIE

Pompey won their first League Cup-tie 2-0 at home to Coventry City on 2 November 1960. The new competition provided some teething problems, as Coventry wanted the match played on a Monday or Tuesday, while Pompey insisted it must be on a Wednesday, as that was early closing day in the city. It was up to clubs to agree between themselves, but in this case the Football League Management Committee intervened, and came down in favour of the home team. A crowd of 5,523 attended the game, and Tony Priscott scored the first goal after three minutes. Ron Saunders netted Pompey's second goal. The Pompey team was: Dick Beattie, Cyril Rutter, Jimmy Dickinson, Ron Howells, Phil Gunter, Harry Harris, Tony Priscott, Ron Saunders, Jimmy White, Sammy Chapman, Ron Newman.

LAST DAY ESCAPE IV

6 May 2001, Division One ....Pompey 3 Barnsley 0

Pompey escaped relegation to Division Two on the last day of the season with an easy victory over Barnsley before a crowd of 17,064. Kevin Miller made a superb save from Lee Bradbury before the striker hammered a close-range shot into the roof of the net on 17 minutes to put Pompey ahead. Steve Lovell should have doubled the lead, but after rounding Miller, he shot wide of the far post. In the 62nd minute, Gary O'Nell grabbed his first senior goal, tapping in a cross from Kevin Harper. Harper then sealed the win, crashing Lovell's cross into the top corner. There was an anxious wait after the final whistle, as fans listened to their radios for results of other matches involved in the relegation issue, but Fratton Park erupted as soon as it was known that Pompey were safe. POMPEY: Aaron Flahavan, Scott Hiley, Jamie Vincent, Linvoy Primus, Carl Tiler, Gary O'Neil, Garry Brady, Lee Sharpe, Kevin Harper, Steve Lovell, Lee Bradbury.

LET'S SHAKE ON IT

On Christmas Day 1957, Pompey's Cyril Rutter ran the length of the field to shake the hand of Chelsea centre-half John Mortimore for scoring an own goal. Rutter had scored in his own net minutes earlier.

A WEDDING SHOE AND A SLIPPER

Pompey centre-forward Alf Strange was married in October 1923. He injured an ankle during Pompey's draw at Brentford the previous week, and had to wear a slipper to his wedding.

JOHN McCARTNEY

John McCartney was Pompey's first manager in the Football League. He arrived immediately after Pompey had won the Southern League Championship in 1920, and promised First Division football in six years. It actually took seven but it was still a great achievement. McCartney had played for Manchester United (in the days when they were known as Newton Heath) Luton Town, and Barnsley, with whom he sustained a knee injury and was forced to retire. He spent three seasons as secretary-manager of the Yorkshire club and then took charge at St. Mirren for six years. At Fratton Park, he soon introduced what he referred to as "the Pompey style", where teamwork rather than individual brilliance was encouraged. The club won the Division Three (South) Championship in 1924, and three years later Pompey were promoted to the First Division. With his dream fulfilled, Mr McCartney resigned on health grounds, and died in 1933.

DICKINSON REMEMBERED

On 19 July 2006, Alton Town Council honoured the memory of Jimmy Dickinson by unveiling a plaque on the wall of 13 Bow Street, the cottage where he was born on 24 April 1925. Dickinson's widow Ann attended the ceremony, along with the couple's son Andrew, daughter-in-law Michelle, and grandsons Edward (9) and Alexander (5), as well as representatives from Portsmouth Football Club.

CHAMPIONSHIP MANAGERS

Ron Saunders and George Graham are the only two former Pompey players to have managed League Championship-winning sides. Saunders achieved the honour with Aston Villa in 1981, and Graham led Arsenal to two titles in 1989 and 1991.

PLAYED IN FA CUP FINALS

Pompey players who have played in FA Cup Finals for other clubs are:

Jack Surtees	West Bromwich Albion	1935
Jimmy Scoular	Newcastle United	1955
Tommy Casey	Newcastle United	1955
Allan Brown	Luton Town	1959
Derek Dougan	Blackburn Rovers	1960
Ray Pointer	Burnley	1962
Jim Standen	West Ham United	1964
Chris Lawler	Liverpool	1965
Jim Storrie	Leeds United	1965
Mike Trebilcock	Everton	1966
Malcolm Manley	Leicester City	1969
George Graham	Arsenal	1971
Peter Mellor	Fulham	1975
Bobby Stokes	Southampton	1976
Paul Mariner	Ipswich Town	1978
Terry Fenwick	Tottenham Hotspur	1982
Micky Hazard	Tottenham Hotspur	1982
Warren Neill	Queens Park Rangers	1982
Steve Foster	Brighton and Hove Albion	1983
Gary Stevens	Brighton and Hove Albion	1983
Dave Beasant	Wimbledon	1988
Neil Webb	Manchester United	1990
Kevin Ball	Sunderland	1992
Paul Hardyman	Sunderland	1992
Paul Merson	Arsenal	1993
David Unsworth	Everton	1995
Teddy Sheringham	Manchester United	1999
Paul Merson	Aston Villa	2000
Sander Westerveld	Liverpool	2001
Patrik Berger	Liverpool	2001
Shaka Hislop	West Ham United	2006

FOREIGN NAMES

Foreign players with names difficult to pronounce are an accepted part of British football today, but they were not so familiar in the 1950s when a Turkish Cypriot joined the Fratton ranks. Ozugh (pronounced Oozay) Ramadan Karayel signed for Pompey on 19 January 1958, and made his debut for Pompey 'A' against local side Andover, but he never made a first-team appearance.

ALL IN THE RESERVES

Following a bad display against Carlisle United at Fratton Park in a Third Division fixture – Pompey lost 2-1 – manager Frank Burrows put the entire first team in the reserves. Whatever the idea was, it failed, because they could only draw 0-0 against an Exeter City reserve side that included five apprentices. The Pompey team was: Alan Knight, John McLaughlin, Steve Bryant, Bobby Doyle, Steve Aizlewood (Peter Ellis), Andy Rollings, Jeff Hemmerman, Steve Berry, Billy Rafferty, Alex Cropley (Alan Rogers), David Crown.

GREAVES RECORD BROKEN

Alan Shearer, at 17 years 220 days, now holds the record as the youngest player to score a hat trick in the First Division. It was previously set by Jimmy Greaves, who scored three times for Chelsea in their 7-4 victory over Pompey at Stamford Bridge on Christmas Day 1957. He was then 17 years 308 days.

TOP OF THE PREMIERSHIP

Pompey went top of the table in August 2003, only three matches after reaching the Premiership. A year to the day since beating Grimsby Town 1-0 to go top of Division One, a win over Bolton Wanderers at Fratton Park would have put Pompey fourth, but a four-goal victory was required to take them to top spot. Goalless at half-time, Steve Stone opened the scoring before Teddy Sheringham's thundering header rounded off a magnificent move. With two minutes to go, Sheringham scored again, and suddenly Pompey were in touching distance of going top of the pile for the first time since January 1952. In the last minute, substitute Vincent Pericard was brought down in the box, and Sheringham completed his hat trick from the spot.

FIRST HAT TRICK IN DIVISION ONE

Jack Smith was the first Pompey player to score a hat trick in the First Division. He achieved the feat on 18 February 1928 against Sunderland at Fratton Park. However, he was not the highest scoring player on the field that day. David Halliday scored four goals for Sunderland, who won 5-3.

POMPEY FINED

In February 2002, Pompey were fined £10,000 for receiving 15 bookings in less than a month.

SUPER-SUB SHERINGHAM

Former Pompey man Teddy Sheringham scored the fastest goal by an England substitute when he netted within ten seconds of coming on against Greece in a World Cup qualifier at Old Trafford on 6 October 2001. Sheringham also scored the quickest goal by a substitute in an FA Cup Final. He grabbed Manchester United's first goal in their 2-0 win over Newcastle United at Wembley in 1999.

TWELVE POINT LEAD

On 24 March 1962, Pompey opened up a 12-point lead over second-placed Bournemouth at the top of the Third Division. It was just as well, as they only managed to pick up one point in the next five matches. Promotion was assured on Easter Monday, when Ron Saunders scored twice at Fratton Park in a 2-1 win over Watford.

ST JOHN PLAYED FOR SCOTLAND

Ian St. John is the only Pompey manager to have played international football for a country other than England. He won 21 Scotland caps and scored nine goals between 1959 and 1965, while his assistant manager at Fratton Park, Billy Hunter, represented the Scots on three occasions.

ALBERT MUNDY

Albert Mundy made 51 League appearances and scored 12 goals for Pompey during the 1950s. He made history after leaving the club by scoring for Aldershot after only six seconds of his side's 3-0 victory away to Hartlepool United in a Division Four fixture on October 25 1958.

NOTHING TO CROWE ABOUT

Jason Crowe made one appearance for Arsenal before his £600,000 transfer to Pompey in the summer of 1999. It came as a substitute against Birmingham City in a League Cup third round tie, and he was sent off after only 33 seconds.

GREGORY FINED AND BANNED

Former Pompey manager John Gregory was fined £7,500, as well as receiving a five-match touchline ban, for abusing the referee in a First Division game at Fratton Park while manager of Derby County in February 2003. His old club beat the Rams 6-2.

QUICK OFF THE MARK

The fastest goal to be scored against Pompey was by Fred Pickering on 24 August 1968. He netted for Birmingham City at St Andrews after 13 seconds of his side's 5-2 victory. In the same match, the Pompey skipper Ron Tindall put through his own goal for the second successive match – he'd also diverted the ball past John Milkins to give Blackburn Rovers a 1-0 victory at Fratton Park three days earlier.

BROKEN FINGER HALTS LONG RUN

Dave Beasant broke a finger while playing for Chelsea against Pompey at Fratton Park in a League Cup third round replay. The injury ended a run of 394 consecutive appearances going back nine years to 29 August 1981.

ANTI-CLIMAX

After a 28-year absence, Pompey were finally promoted to the First Division on 5 May 1987, less than 48 hours short of the 60th anniversary of their elevation to the top flight in 1927. However, promotion was something of an anti-climax, as Pompey were not involved in a match. Oldham Athletic had a chance of sneaking into the promotion frame, but their 2-0 defeat away to Shrewsbury Town meant Pompey had reached Division One. There was still a chance that Pompey could finish as champions, but on the last day of the season, leaders Derby County beat Plymouth Argyle 4-2 at the Baseball Ground while Pompey slumped to a 2-1 defeat at home to Sheffield United.

HARRY WALKER

Harry Walker, who played in goal for Pompey in the 1939 FA Cup Final, was arguably the most agile goalkeeper the club have ever had. His one weakness, though, was his kicking. With the wind against him, his goalkicks hardly left the penalty area, so his full-backs usually did the honours for him.

HALF AN OWN GOAL

Jack Froggatt entered the record books as being the scorer of half an own goal on 18 December 1954. The former Pompey hero attempted to clear the ball while playing for Leicester City, but Stan Milburn touched it at the same time, and instead of being cleared to safety the ball flew into the Leicester net. As neither player wanted to claim sole responsibility, it went down officially as a Froggatt and Milburn own goal.

YOUNG GUN'S LOAN SPELL

Lee Sharpe, who spent three months on loan with Pompey in 2000/01, was once the youngest player to represent the England under-21 side. He was 17 years and 254 days when he played in the 1-0 defeat against Greece at Patras.

ALF STRANGE

Alf Strange was the first of only two players – Peter Harris being the other – to score five goals in a match for Pompey. He had not been a great success at centre-forward prior to his fantastic five-goal feat in January 1923, and the majority of supporters wanted him to be dropped for the visit of Gillingham in a Third Division (South) fixture. However, Strange responded by scoring a first-half hat trick, and then added two more goals after the half-time interval. In November 1925, he was transferred to Port Vale, and it was at Vale Park that a switch of positions dramatically changed his career. He moved to right-half, and was soon snapped up by Sheffield Wednesday. He won two League Championships, in 1929 and 1930, while at Hillsborough, and was capped 20 times for England.

TOP GOALSCORERS V

Pompey's top League goal-scorers between 1988/89 and 2005/06 were:

1988/89	Mick Quinn	18
1989/90	Guy Whittingham	23
1990/91	Colin Clarke and Martin Kuhl	13
1991/92	Guy Whittingham	11
1992/93	Guy Whittingham	42
1993/94	Gerry Creaney	11
1994/95	Gerry Creaney	18
1995/96	Alan McLoughlin	10
1996/97	Lee Bradbury	15
1997/98	John Aloisi	12
1998/99	John Aloisi	14
1999/00	Steve Claridge	14
2000/01	Steve Claridge	11
2001/02	Peter Crouch	18
2002/03	Svetoslav Todorov	26
2003/04	Yakubu Ayegbeni	16
2004/05	Yakubu Ayegbeni	12
2005/06	Lomana LuaLua	7

UP TO THE PREMIERSHIP

Pompey won the First Division title in 2002/03. They began with a 2-0 home win over Nottingham Forest, went top on 26 August following a 1-0 victory at Grimsby Town, and never looked back. Skippered by Paul Merson, the team broke three club records and equalled another. They scored 97 goals, collected 98 points, and won 29 matches. They also equalled the club record of 11 away victories. Promotion was secured with a 1-0 victory at home to Burnley, and they made certain of the title by beating Rotherham United 3-2 at Fratton Park.

Football League Division One 2002/03

	Pl	W	D	L	F	A	W	D	L	F	A	Pts
1 POMPEY	46	17	3	3	52	22	12	8	3	45	23	98
2 Leicester City	46	16	5	2	40	12	10	9	4	33	28	92
3 Sheffield United	46	13	7	3	38	23	10	4	9	34	29	80
4 Reading	46	13	3	7	33	21	12	1	10	28	25	79
5 Wolverhampton W.	46	9	10	4	40	19	11	6	6	41	25	76
6 Nottingham F	46	14	7	2	57	23	6	7	10	25	27	74
7 Ipswich Town	46	10	5	8	49	39	9	8	6	31	25	70
8 Norwich City	46	14	4	5	36	17	5	8	10	24	32	69
9 Millwall	46	11	6	6	34	32	8	3	12	25	37	66
10 Wimbledon	46	12	5	6	39	28	6	6	11	37	45	65
11 Gillingham	46	10	6	7	33	31	6	8	9	23	34	62
12 Preston North End	46	11	7	5	44	29	5	6	12	24	41	61
13 Watford	46	11	5	7	33	26	6	4	13	21	44	60
14 Crystal Palace	46	8	10	5	29	17	6	7	10	30	35	59
15 Rotherham United	46	8	9	6	27	25	7	5	11	35	37	59
16 Burnley	46	10	4	9	35	44	5	6	12	30	45	55
17 Walsall	46	10	3	10	34	34	5	6	12	23	35	54
18 Derby County	46	9	5	9	33	32	6	2	15	22	42	52
19 Bradford City	46	7	8	8	27	35	7	2	14	24	38	52
20 Coventry City	46	6	6	11	23	31	6	8	9	23	31	50
21 Stoke City	46	9	6	8	25	25	3	8	12	20	44	50
22 Sheffield Wednesday	46	7	7	9	29	32	3	9	11	27	41	46
23 Brighton	46	7	6	10	29	31	4	6	13	20	36	45
24 Grimsby Town	46	5	6	12	26	39	4	6	13	22	46	39

FIRST GOAL CONCEDED

When Bobby Barclay put Huddersfield Town ahead against Pompey in the 1939 FA Cup semi-final at Highbury, it was the first goal Pompey had conceded in that year's competition.

LAST 40,000 GATE

The last time Fratton Park housed a 40,000-plus gate for a League match was on 23 August 1958, when West Ham United were the visitors on the opening day of the season. The crowd of 40,470 saw the Hammers celebrate their return to the First Division after a period of 26 years by beating Pompey 2-1. Vic Keeble and Johnny Dick gave the Londoners a 2-0 lead before Peter Harris pulled a goal back for Pompey.

FAMILY DAY

Following the success of Ladies' Day at Fratton Park, Jimmy Dickinson, in his role as Public Relations Officer, organized a Family Day in 1966. The club's gymnasium was turned into a children's crèche so that couples could leave the children in the care of Mrs Ann Dickinson and her team of helpers. The Royal Navy supplied the equipment for the children. The day was such a success that the crèche continued for some years.

TWO JOHN McLAUGHLINS

Two men with the name John McLaughlin have played for Pompey. The first was a midfield player who played five games on loan from Liverpool during the 1975/76 season. The second John McLaughlin was from Swindon Town, and he made 179 league and cup appearances – all in the right-back position – between 1979 and 1984.

SHEARER BREAKS TOON RECORD

Alan Shearer broke Newcastle United's all-time goalscoring record in a Premiership fixture against Pompey at St. James' Park on 4 February 2006. He scored the Magpies' second goal in the 64th minute of their 2-0 win.

O'NEIL'S THE YOUNGEST

Gary O'Neil became the youngest player to play for Pompey when he appeared as substitute in a First Division match against Barnsley on 29 January 2000. He was aged 16 years 256 days, beating the record previously held by Andy Awford, who was 16 years 275 days when he made his debut away to Crystal Palace on 15 April 1989.

TWO MBEs

Two Pompey players have been awarded MBEs – Jimmy Dickinson in 1964 and Alan Knight in 2001.

ENGLAND CAREER CURTAILED

Len Phillips would have won more than three England caps had it not been for a freak injury sustained while training with the national team. When playing a simple back-pass in a practice match at The Valley, he stubbed the ground and injured his knee. This robbed him of a place on a Continental tour that same year, and also effectively ended his league career.

GORDON'S HAT TRICK

Johnny Gordon scored over 100 goals in two spells with Pompey, but only managed one hat trick. It came against Sheffield Wednesday at Hillsborough on 24 October 1953, and helped Pompey to a 4-4 draw. His first goal brought Pompey level at 2-2, and then, with his side 4-2 behind, he struck twice in the last 15 minutes.

ALL-TIME TOP GOALSCORERS

Three former Pompey players top the all-time goalscoring charts with different clubs.

314 ....John Atyeo ....Bristol City...................................1951-1966
203 ....Ray Crawford ....Ipswich Town 1958-1963, 1966-1969
93 ....Teddy Sheringham........Millwall...1984-1991

GRAHAM'S DOUBLE TREBLE

Former Pompey player George Graham is the only player to win all three domestic trophies as a player and manager. He won a League Cup winners' medal with Chelsea in 1965, when the Blues beat Leicester City 3-2 over two legs; was a member of the Arsenal 1970/71 League and FA Cup double-winning side; and as a manager, led Arsenal to the League Championship in 1989 and 1991, and to FA Cup and League Cup success in 1993.

TOP OF THE TABLE

Pompey went top of the First Division in September 1936 following a 2-1 win at home to Manchester City. They held the position for two months, dropping to second after a 4-0 defeat by Everton at Goodison Park on 21 November. A 1-1 draw at home to Bolton Wanderers put them back on top, but another 4-0 reverse, at Brentford the following week, saw them slip to third. They finished the season in ninth place, and didn't reach top spot again until 4 September 1948, when a Peter Harris goal earned a 1-0 victory away to Stoke City.

HONOURS DEGREE FOR KNIGHT

In 1996, Alan Knight was awarded an honorary Master of Science degree by Portsmouth University in recognition of his service to Portsmouth Football Club and the community.

ENGLAND YOUTH CAPTAIN SENT OFF

Ian Hendon, who spent a month on loan from Tottenham Hotspur during the 1992/93 campaign, captained England Youth against Czechoslovakia at Fratton Park in November 1989 – and was sent off shortly before half-time.

CLIFF PARKER

Cliff Parker starred for Pompey either side of the war. He joined Pompey from Doncaster Rovers in December 1933 and, once established in the Pompey line-up, he hardly missed a game until the outbreak of war. He was a wonderful crosser of the ball, and it was said he was capable of dropping a ball on a sixpence. A gentleman off the field, he was totally fearless on it and was often in trouble of his own making. This may be why international honours passed him by. His greatest moment came in 1939, when he scored twice at Wembley as Pompey beat Wolverhampton Wanderers 4-1 in the FA Cup Final. He was still a fixture in the side during the first post-war season of 1946/47, and he made a valuable contribution to the double League Championship success of 1948/49 and 1949/50, continuing to be a member of the playing staff until 1953, when he was appointed chief scout. In May 1954, he became assistant trainer and continued in the role until 1957.

RELIEF ON CENTENARY DAY

Pompey met Birmingham City on 4 April 1998 in Division One, 100 years all but one day since the formation of the club. Many former players were invited, and the match was a vital one, since Pompey were on the brink of relegation to the Second Division. A defeat looked certain when Dele Adebola gave the visitors an 87th-minute 1-0 lead, but Pompey defender Andy Thomson popped up in the last minute to stab home the equaliser.

A LOT OF GOALKEEPERS

When Yoshi Kawaguchi made his Pompey debut in October 2001, he was the sixth player to play in goal for Pompey in 22 league matches. The other five were: Aaron Flahavan, Andy Petterson, Chris Tardif, Sasa Ilic, and Dave Beasant.

CHERRETT'S DEBUT GOAL

Percy Cherrett was transferred from Pompey to Plymouth Argyle on 28 August 1923, and scored on his debut against his old team-mates in a Third Division (South) fixture at Home Park.

BIG LET-DOWN

One of the most disappointing FA Cup performances in Pompey's history occurred in January 1976, when Charlton Athletic beat them in a fourth round replay at Fratton Park. Bottom of Division Two, they had won 1-0 away to First Division Birmingham City in the third round, and forced a 1-1 draw with Charlton at The Valley. A bumper crowd of 31,722 turned up at Fratton to witness the most inept display seen from a Pompey team for years. It was goalless at half-time, but 15 minutes into the second half the visitors were 2-0 ahead. By the time they scored their third goal five minutes from time, thousands had already left.

LONG-AWAITED VICTORIES

Below is a list of teams over whom an away win is long overdue (as at August 2006), along with the result and date of Pompey's last away victory.

20/08/1949 ....3-1 v Newcastle United ....Division One
19/10/1957 ....3-0 v Manchester United ....Division One
05/11/1955 ....3-1 v Sheffield United ....Division One
17/09/1955 ....3-1 v Arsenal ....Division One
03/09/1955 ....5-1 v Chelsea ....Division One
02/09/1961 ....1-0 v Queens Park Rangers ....Division Three

GREGORY OUT PROTEST

About 20 Pompey supporters demonstrated outside Martin Gregory's home in December 1998, the last month of the club's centenary year. The protestors took with them a letter from the Independent Supporters' Club to Gregory. It criticised the handling of the latest financial crisis and urged him to leave. One banner said, "Proud Pompey, 100 years old and dying courtesy of Mr Gregory."

TIP FOR THE TELEGRAM BOY

In 1949, 15-year-old John Wearne delivered a telegram telling Jack Froggatt he had been picked for England. The surprised Froggatt gave the boy two shillings (10p).

THE CHURCH MAG

Phil Gunter was a lay preacher, and was a regular contributor to the local church magazine. He greatly upset his manager at Pompey, Freddie Cox, when he criticised his management in one of his articles.

THREE MINUTES FROM WEMBLEY

Pompey haven't taken part in an FA Cup Final since 1939, but how close they came in 1992. On 5 April, the club's 95th birthday, they met Liverpool in the semi-final at Highbury, and took the mighty Reds to extra time. There was no doubt they had been the better side over the 90 minutes, and finally took a deserved lead through Darren Anderton in the second half of extra time. With only three minutes remaining, Andy Awford chopped down John Barnes just outside the box. The Liverpool man took the kick himself. It hit a post, and rebounded to Ronnie Whelan, who smashed home the equaliser. The replay was at Villa Park eight days later, and once again the score was goalless after 90 minutes, but shortly before the end Pompey's Alan McLoughlin had hit the bar from six yards. It remained 0-0 at the end of extra-time, and for the first time in history an FA Cup semi-final was decided on a penalty shoot-out. Liverpool won 3-1 on penalties, and went on to lift the trophy. It could have been Pompey.

THE JIMMY ALLEN STAND

The sale of Jimmy Allen to Aston Villa for £10,775 in June 1934 was at the time a record fee for a defender, and only £115 short of the British transfer record. The money Pompey received meant they had made a profit of £14,961 for the year, and the transfer fee went to building the North Stand, raising the capacity to 58,000 with covering for 33,000. The Stand was opened on 7 September 1935 by John McKenna, President of the Football League when, coincidentally, Aston Villa were the visitors. When Jimmy Allen led the Villa team onto the pitch, the band struck up with, "Dear Old Pal". In 1988, the stand was re-cladded and while work was in progress, 78-year-old Jimmy Allen made a sentimental trip to view what was for many years referred to in jovial fashion as "the Jimmy Allen Stand".

HARRY REDKNAPP

Harry Redknapp was the third manager to lead Pompey into the top flight. In the summer of 2001, after departing as manager of West Ham, he turned down several offers of management to become Director of Football at Fratton Park. Nine months later, he took over from Graham Rix, and little more than a year on, Pompey had won the First Division title.

TERRY VENABLES

Terry Venables spent a mysterious year-and-a-half with Pompey from August 1997 to December 1998. It was never quite clear to supporters what his role was, although he was named as chairman after supposedly buying the club from the Gregory family for £1.

VELIMIR ZAJEC

Velimir Zajec was brought to Fratton Park in November 2004 by Milan Mandaric as Director of Football. It was the beginning of great upheaval – Harry Redknapp resigned, and soon became manager of Southampton. Zajec acted as manager and at first results were favourable, but by April a return to the First Division looked highly possible. Alain Perrin was brought in as manager, and relegation was avoided, but Zajec never started the job he was brought in to do, and left early into the new season.

SEMI-FINAL PLACE AFTER 43 YEARS

Pompey reached the FA Cup semi-final in 1992 for the first time in 43 years by beating Nottingham Forest 1-0 in the sixth round at Fratton Park. Alan McLoughlin poked home the only goal from six yards after only three minutes.

MULTI-NATIONAL SQUAD

Pompey embarked on life as a Premiership club in 2003 with the following multi-national squad:

Australia	Hayden Foxe
Bulgaria	Svetoslav Todorov
Croatia	Boris Zivkovic
Czech Republic	Patrik Berger
England	several
France	Vincent Pericard
Holland	Arjan de Zeeuw, Harald Wapenaar
Japan	Yoshikatsu Kawaguchi
Nigeria	Yakubu Ayegbeni
Scotland	several
Senegal	Amdy Faye
Serbia & Montenegro	Dejan Stefanovic
Trinidad & Tobago	Shaka Hislop
Wales	Carl Robinson